INFORMATION AND SOCIETY SERIES

Transnational Data Flows in the Information Age

Cees J Hamelink

DATE DUE

Edited by

Transnational Data Reportir
Amsterdam, The Netherland

Studentlitteratur AE
Chartwell-Bratt Ltd.

Cover: Kjeld Brandt
© Cees J Hamelink, 1984
Printed in Sweden
Studentlitteratur
Lund 1984
ISBN 91-44-20621-6 (Studentlitteratur)
ISBN 0-86238-042-1 (Chartwell–Bratt)

Table of contents

Preface

At the beginning of this decade the MacBride Commission presented to UNESCO the results of its enquiries into the complexities of the world's communication problems. Whatever its shortcomings may be, the Commission's work definitely legitimized the communication/information field as an area of serious and urgent academic and political attention. Consequently, 1980 stands out as a crucial time in a process that dates back to the late 1960s and that will undoubtedly occupy our minds into the 1990s.

Nineteen-eighty-three is World Communications Year. Other important events are approaching, such as the second World Conference on Strategies and Policies for Informatics (SPIN II). On the way to the ominous 1984, this may offer a stimulus for reflection on the question of to what extent Orwell's projections of all-embracing telecommunications control are indeed coming true!

This study is about the most potent form of telecommunication: transnational data flows. It sets out to describe the main actors and their impact on society. The context of the analysis is the 'information age': the recognition that information is becoming society's major operative factor.

It deserves acknowledgement that part of the research material for this book stems from work initially prepared under a contract with the United Nations Centre on Transnational Corporations. Special thanks for their comments and suggestions are also due to Herbert Schiller and Russell Pipe. I want to mention my affiliation with the Institute of Social Studies since its staff and facilities provide such a stimulating environment for creative labour.

Cees J Hamelink

Introduction

Data

In recent years debates on global political and economic issues have been enriched with such new concepts as data trade, data barrier, data war, data haven, data drain, data inspection and data law.

All these 'neologisms' refer to the increasing importance of the movement of data across national borders. As France's Minister of Industry, André Giraud, has observed, "This transfrontier data flow is increasing rapidly and playing an ever greater part in the organisation of production and international trade."[1] The flow of data across borders (Transnational Data Flow) causes considerable anxiety for national politicians and transnational industrialists.

On the national political level it is feared that a totally uncontrolled flow of data could present a serious threat to indigenous cultural identity, political independence and the balance of payment. As the chairman of the Brazilian delegation to a world conference of the Intergovernmental Bureau for Informatics (IBI) claimed, "It is fundamental that a country have control over the information resources essential to its sovereignty and development." Consequently, "an effective control over foreign trade of information" would be necessary.[2]

On the level of transnational business, it is feared that any restriction on the free flow of data would seriously hinder effective commercial operations. As the director for telecommunication regulatory policy at the Bank of America states, "It's simple: if we can't move information, we go out of business."[3]

In spite of the 'neologisms' and the current anxieties, transnational data flow is in itself not a brand new phenomenon. Since the dawn of mankind's history data of different kinds have been collected, transported and processed. Early examples come from reports about Roman emperors travelling abroad accompanied by their mobile 'data banks' – card registers with data on Roman citizens.

Also the history of science provides numerous instances of data collection and data processing carried out in geographically distant locations.

Over the centuries data have been collected for military, diplomatic, commercial, religious or artistic reasons and carried across great distances through various support media for their processing in locations different from the places of origin. One characteristic unites all these widely varying data: they are all the basic components – the 'raw materials' as it were – of information.

Data represent facts, concepts and their relations in a format that is suitable for processing. Through a set of operations (either with the human mind or by machine equipment) data can be organized into functional information.

Data are, for example, the *fact* that the sun rises in the orient and sets in the occident, the *concepts:* sun, rise, set, orient and occident, and the *relations* between these concepts. As such, these data have a limited significance. One could say that their meaning is restricted to their own closed 'inner world'. Processing such data is their placement in a wider context; they become related to the 'outer world' of geographical patterns, the shape of the globe, flood and ebb tide, night and day, time, life, etc. They become part of a total that has meaning for various dimensions of human behaviour.

What today is referred to as transnational data flow has a distinct feature in that the data flows are streams of binary digits carried across borders on such media as magnetic tapes, discs and punch cards or through telecommunication circuits, and processed by electronic computers. This implies at least a drastic quantitative change vis-à-vis earlier data flows and their processing. The application of the electronic computer and advanced telecommunication carriers – and particularly the convergence of these techniques – has facilitated an exponential increase of volume, speed and reliability of both transport and processing.

Over the past decades increasingly sophisticated equipment has been developed for the collecting of data about natural and social phenomena. An example is the high-quality photographic equipment used in remote resource-sensing satellites. This is an indication of the fact that data are considered so valuable as to legitimize the investments for such equipment. Similarly, more refined machinery has been developed for the transformation of data into functional information. The development of computer intelligence can actually be seen as a constant search to increase the volume and complexity of manipulations that can be performed on data. Through such manipulations more value is added to the data.

This is reflected in the distinction that the United Nations Committee on the Peaceful Uses of Outer Space (COPUOS) has proposed between primary data (collected through satellites and not yet processed) and analyzed information (the product after processing).[4] The primary data are being collected on all countries by the NASA Landsat satellites and are disseminated at very low prices. The analyzed information, however, is considered proprietary information and is sold at much higher prices.

Information

The significance of data is given with the fact that they are information's key resource. And without information social development is impossible. All its dimensions – be they agriculture, health care, education or mineral exploitation – are based on flows of information. They all involve decisions about the allocation of a society's physical and human resources, and in any decision-making process information is a central component.

Information is important in decision-making because it makes alternatives known and reduces the uncertainty about the implications of an alternative.

This function of information can be derived from the different mathematical, biological and quantum-physical models that have been developed for the definition of information.[5]

When the concept 'information' is used in the abundance of literature describing it, there is generally an important reference to the mathematical information theory (or telecommunication theory) of Shannon and Weaver. Thereby it is not unusual to ignore that this is in fact a chapter from the theory of probabilities which points to the probability with which a minimal number of signals can transport a maximum of information items. The Shannon/ Weaver theory does not go beyond a linear transportation model which does not actually formulate what 'information' is. However, their theory established some general characteristics which are helpful in the definition of information.

In the line of the probability model information presupposes a previous situation of uncertainty, and the greater the uncertainty, the smaller the probability of the occurrence of a certain possible signal and the more information this signal contains. This relating of information to the unpredictable occurrence of signals in an uncertain situation is taken much further in the quantum theory. There the impossibility to predict the movement of the elementary particles created so-called 'single' alternatives, i.e. every next move is equally probable and can only be fixed when indeed the next location is established and thus the uncertainty eliminated.

Accordingly, information can be formulated as exactly that degree of growth of knowledge and experience gained by a given event because a given number of previously completely undetermined but equally probable single alternatives will be determined by this process, thus decreasing the degree of former insecurity. Further meaning can be given to this from the biological model of an open information system – the macromolecule DNA: carrier of the genetic characteristics. This is a control system which is involved in a continuous feedback process with its environment. Especially relevant here is the knowledge that the DNA chains in their genetic code contain the whole complexity of possible types of organisms in a reduction which can be termed 'information about information'. One should observe, however, that the complexity is reduced not by the information *per se,* but by its organisation. It should also be noted that 'information about information' implies that the information contains indications for information to be generated beyond its own content.

In summary, it can be said that from the mathematical, biological and quantum-physical models information can be defined as: 'unpredictable signals which at their occurrence eliminate the uncertain choice between possible alternatives, thus reducing complexity (by organisation in basic categories) and indicating what can be generated beyond their specific content'.

Information and society

The transformation of data – myriads of impulses that human beings receive constantly – into 'information' is critical for the adaptation to the environment. The physical and social environment demands continuous and adequate responses. With increasing adequacy chances for survival increase significantly.

There is a constant offering of equally probable alternatives between which choices have to be made.

The process of adaptation can be seriously hindered if there is an over-stimulation, an overload of data. 'Overload' causes hindrances for human observation, thinking and deciding.

The possible intake of impulses (data) is restricted by the physiological capacities of each organism. Each organism needs a certain time span for the transportation of incoming signals through its nervous system. Although human organisms carry signals some 30,000 cms. in a second, the capacity for data processing is limited and can cause strong disturbances in the confrontation with quickly changing, very complex environments.

Highly industrialised societies, in particular, create such environments and demand appropriate mechanisms for the fast and accurate organisation of data into information.

The finding that information at its occurrence eliminates uncertain choices between alternative possibilities and reduces thus the complexity of the environment can be applied to social systems.

In every society allocative decisions have to be taken and information is an essential input in this process. As studies about social decision-making show, the exchange of information is integrally related to the distribution of power in a given society.[6] Those who control the formal, institutional channels of information exchange (such as the public media) will have better chances to determine which information is the most crucial, which information represents the decisive alternative in choices that have to be made. They play a greater part in the definition of a society's 'agenda' than those that are prohibited from making inputs and that have smaller chance to 'influence' others to accept their alternative.

Participation in exchanges of information and consequently the degree of influence on decision-making has during the past decade come to be recognized as a crucial dimension in international relations.

Developing countries in particular have pointed at this in their demand for a restructuring of international information structures. On various occasions the international community has recognized this and endorsed the establishment of a new international information order as a logical corollary to the establishment of a new international economic order.[7]

A growing body of research evidence supports the existence of large discrepancies in the informational capacities of developed and developing countries.[8]

An important question therefore is whether the current flows of computerized data across borders could be seen as adding yet another component to this well documented and internationally recognized phenomenon. This is important because present global information discrepancies are crucial factors in the hampering of autonomous and self-reliant development in developing countries.[9]

13

Pursuing independent development creates for developing countries new information requirements. They need access to information and input of information that reflect the alternative choices that meet their needs and priorities.

The question then is whether through transnational data flows developing countries have greater or lesser access to information that is pertinent to their development and whether they provide developing countries with more or less chances to participate in the international information exchange.

Formulated in more operational terms: is decision-making capacity vis-à-vis the management of national resources located extra-territorially through transnational data flows? Or, can transnational data flows strengthen national capacity for decision-making about the management of resources?

These questions have to be explored in the context of present users and applications of transnational data flows. As will be indicated later, current transnational data flows are to a significant degree tied up with the activities of transnational industrial and financial corporations.

A growing body of literature documents the important role of these corporations in the international economy and the domestic economies of both their home and host countries.[10] Their role is particularly related to their capacity to decisively influence resource allocation.

Transnational corporations are highly information-intensive due to their organisation and strategy. They nowadays also become 'increasingly dependent upon worldwide computer circuits.'[11] "The complexity of international business today places a premium on speed and accuracy."[12] Transnational corporations are thus faced with 'communication problems that demand sophisticated technological solutions.'[13] Transnational data flows offer such sophisticated technological solutions. Consequently, a vital question becomes, do transnational data flows increase the informational advantage and social impact of transnational corporations?

Lack of data

The questions asked in the preceding paragraphs cannot be satisfactorily answered in the present study. Although one finds an abundance of statements on the significance of transnational data flows, the empirical material that one would need is not available.

As a document prepared by the Intergovernmental Bureau for Informatics remarks, there is "little in the way of appraising the real value of a transnational corporation's information resources or the value of its ability to rapidly transmit data internally to any other organisational unit. Neither qualitative nor quantitative measurements of internal corporate data transactions seem to exist or are available."[14]

Data are difficult to obtain for a number of reasons:

- Inasmuch as data are transported by mail service, the confidentiality of correspondence makes it impossible for PTTs to calculate data volumes.
- Much of data traffic takes place through public-switched telephone networks which give no disaggregate information about data and other traffic.
- Data carried across borders on material-support media (discs, cards, tapes) give problems because customs statistics do not disaggregate data traffic and computer materials.
- Moreover, the data traffic one would want to measure relates to the core of corporate operations, their R&D activities, their organisation and marketing. Corporate management may therefore not feel very sympathetic to the researchers' needs.[15] Additionally, in many cases the firms themselves simply do not have such information.

The scope of this study is consequently limited. It will mainly attempt to produce and analyze the available documentation with which the key questions can be defined and refined as the points of departure for policy and planning in this crucial field.

Notes Introduction

1 A. Giraud (Minister of Industry, France) in an address at the OECD High Level Conference on Information, Computer and Communications Policies for the 1980s, Paris, October 6–8, 1980.
2 Joubert de Oliveira Brízida, address at the IBI World Conference on Transborder Data Flow Policies, Rome, June 23–27, 1980.
3 B. C. Burgess, quoted in *The Wall Street Journal,* August 26, 1981.
4 J. F. Gunther, *The United States and the Debate on the World Information Order,* Washington: Academy for Educational Development, 1979, p 2.
5 *Cf.* C. E. Shannon and W. Weaver, *The Mathematical Theory of Communication,* Urbana, 1949; F. Solms, *Towards an Ecumenical Network of Information Systems*; Geneva: Lutheran World Federation, 1974; C. F. von Weizsäcker, 'Materie, Energie und Information', in idem (ed), *Die Einheit der Natur,* Munich, 1971.

6 *Cf.* J. E. Grunig, 'Communication in Community Decisions on the Problems of the Poor', in *The Journal of Communication,* Vol 22, 1972, pp 5–25.

7 *I.a.* Twentieth General Conference of UNESCO, Paris, November 1978; UNESCO-IBI SPIN Conference, Torremolinos, September 1978; United Nations General Assembly, New York, December 18, 1978; Twenty-First General Conference of UNESCO, Belgrade, October 1980.

8 Much of the research in this field has been compiled in the Final Report of the UNESCO-sponsored International Commission for the Study of Communication Problems, *Many Voices, One World,* Paris, UNESCO, 1980, in particular Part II (Chapter 6) and Part III (Chapter 1).

9 C. J. Hamelink, *Cultural Autonomy in Global Communications,* New York, Longman, 1983.

10 For a review see: *Research on Transnational Corporations,* United Nations (E/C. 10/12) January 1976; and *Les sociétés transnationales dans le développement mondial: un reexamen,* United Nations Centre on Transnational Corporations, 1978.

11 Report of the Carter Administration to the US House of Representatives Committee on International Operations and the US Senate Committee on Commerce, Science and Transportation, quoted by *Computerworld,* February 19, 1979.

12 R. B. White, Vice-president of Citibank, in his testimony during the Hearings before the US Senate Sub-committee on International Operations of the US Senate Committee on Foreign Relations, Washington, 1977.

13 *Ibidem.*

14 Intergovernmental Bureau for Informatics, *Transborder Data Flow: its environment and consequences,* SPIN document 231, Rome, June 1980, p 55.

15 *Cf.* the study on Data Security and Confidentiality, carried out for the Commission of the European Communities and submitted in 1980, "Thus, the data we were requesting were often considered confidential by those we interviewed who, in many cases, refused to give them to us, or demanded a written guarantee that we would treat the information in confidence," quoted in *Transnational Data Report,* Vol III No 2, 1980, p 8.

1 The Information Age

Advanced industrialized countries in the latter part of the twentieth century are often characterized by referring to the concept of informatisation. These countries are described as 'information societies', their economies have become 'information economies', their 'informatisation' grows rapidly, and they are in the midst of 'information explosions' and 'information revolutions'.

And – as some observers add – also countries that are less advanced, such as the newly industrializing countries, are well on their way to joining the 'informatised world'.[1]

In a general sense, these information-linked descriptions are used to indicate that 'information handling' (i.e. the generating, processing, storing and transmitting of information) delivers an ever larger contribution to a country, in terms of the percentage of the Gross National Product it yields and the labour force it needs. The descriptions suggest a country's dependence upon the resource information which more and more outweighs the role of the strategic resources of primarily agricultural and industrial societies. They reflect the observation that the significance of information has become comparable to raw materials in the agricultural society or capital in the industrial society. They also claim that the technology of information handling will increasingly underlie all production and distribution of goods and services, like muscular strength in the agricultural society and energy in the industrial society.

Bell, Porat, Nora-Minc

In his perceptive analysis of the transitory nature of the industrial society, Daniel Bell projected what he termed the 'post-industrial society'.[2]

For this society he acknowledged the importance of information by stating, "And if capital and labour are the major structural features of industrial society, information and knowledge are those of the post-industrial society."[3]

To support this insight that information activities are the crucial elements in the transformation towards a post-industrial society, a study by Marc Uri Porat did provide a large volume of empirical data.[4]

Porat's study delineates a 'primary information sector' in the US economy which comprises knowledge production and inventive industries, information distribution and communication industries, risk management, search and coordination industries, information processing and transmission services, information goods industries, selected government activities (such as postal services) and various support services (such as office furnishing). The data indicate that already in 1967 this sector generated over 25% of the Gross National Product.[5]

This finding implies for Porat the necessity to discuss 'what it means for the US to evolve from an economy that is based primarily on manufacturing and industry to one that is based primarily on knowledge, communication and information'.[6]

In studies by the OECD, carried out during 1972 and 1973 in Sweden, France, the Federal Republic of Germany and England, the results come close to Porat's data. It is found that approximately 30% of the Gross National Product in these countries stems from the primary information sector.

Also, in a study commissioned by the French government, information activities are found to be a crucial factor in present social developments.[7] This study, by Simon Nora and Alain Minc, sees at the heart of the crisis that France faces the 'informatisation' of society. The rapidly expanding 'informatics revolution', amply documented in the supporting material of the study, is considered today's gravest challenge for French society. It 'will modify the nerve centre of the whole society'.[8]

Information age

A very appropriate concept to summarize social developments in which information handling is the major operative factor is the 'information age'. It recognizes more adequately than such concepts as 'information society' or 'information economy' that there are also other pertinent factors at work, such as nuclear energy. It does not reduce the analysis of society to one comprehensive notion, but proposes that in the present state of transition an essential factor is the volume and capacity of a country's information handling.[9]

Information age indicates thus the relative importance of information handling in a given country. It is comparable to the historical existence of the 'bronze age', for example. This age in which bronze was the key material for the construction of essential tools did occur in different locations at different times. With the emergence of a new age, the 'iron age', it disappeared.

The same applies to the information age. It occurs in different parts of the world at different times and may phase out again with the coming of yet another 'age'.

Therefore, one could locate countries on a continuous scale which moves from less information handling to more information handling. The score on the continuum would indicate whether and to which extent a country has entered the information age.

Measuring the information age

The Japanese Research Institute for Telecommunications and Economics (RITE) has devised an 'index of informatisation'. It used basically four composite factors: the amount of information, the information equipment, the information processing capacity, and a coefficient of information (see Table I).

The index was applied in the Japanese Ministry of Post and Telecommunications' 'White Paper on Communications for 1975'. It showed a considerable increase in Japan's annual average rate of growth in informatisation: between 1965 and 1973 this was 10%.[10]

The index was also used for cross-national comparisons between Japan, the US, England, France and the Federal Republic of Germany.[11] In general the results showed that between 1965 and 1973 the index of informatisation in these countries almost doubled.

Following the Japanese initiative it seems desirable to design and apply an index of measuring the information age that is more comprehensive. Such an index is proposed in Table II and encompasses forty items (extending the eleven items of the RITE index) which are grouped under the composite factors of information-handling volume, information-handling capacity and level of information handling.[12]

In Table III some illustrations are given of the growth of certain items in the index over the past years.

Table I The RITE Information Index

A. Composite Factor: Information Quantity

Items
1) Number of letters mailed per inhabitant
2) Number of phone calls per inhabitant
3) Daily circulation of newspapers per 100 inhabitants
4) Production of books

B. Composite Factor: Information Equipment

Items
5) Population per square kilometer
6) Number of telephones per 100 inhabitants
7) Number of tv receivers per 100 inhabitants
8) Number of computers per 100 inhabitants

C. Composite Factor: Level of Information Processing Capacity

Items
9) Percentage of persons employed in tertiary sector
10) Number of university students per 100 inhabitants

D. Information Coefficient

Items
11) Percentage of personal income for miscellaneous expenditure

Table II Composite Information-Handling Index

I Information-Handling Volume	II Information-Handling Capacity	III Level of Information Handling

A. Volume of Information Supply
1) circulation daily newspapers
2) circulation weekly newspapers
3) circulation spec. magazines
4) tv hours per day
5) book production
6) library holdings
 	
B. Volume of Information Demand
7) letters mailed per inhabitant
8) phone calls per inhabitant
9) library loans per inhabitant
10) subscriptions dailies
11) telex traffic
12) hours spent with tv
13) data base searches
 	
C. Information Occupations
14) % information-linked jobs
 	
D. Information Industry
15) telecom.services
16) dp industry
17) news production
18) book publishing
19) consumer electronics
20) advertising
	A. Information Equipment
	21) number of telephones
	22) number of radio sets
	23) number of tv sets
	24) number of computers
	25) number of libraries
	26) number of data bases
	
	B. Information Investment
	27) for telecommunication
	28) for informatics
	
	C. Information Expenditure
	29) private expenditure for various
	    subscriptions
	30) private expenditure for
	    information equipment
	
	D. Access to Equipment
	31) capacity computers
	32) capacity telecom.equip.
	33) capacity tv sets
		A. Information Education
		34) schools of journalism
		35) radio/tv training
		36) informatics training
		37) library/documentation training
		
		B. Information Specialists
		38) mass media staff
		39) informaticians
		40) information technology engineers

Table III Some Illustrations of Information Index Growth

Information Supply

Daily Circulation Newspapers per 100 inhabitants

	1965	1972
Japan	45	52
US	31	30
England	48	53
Fed. Rep. of Germany	33	29
France	25	33

Information Demand

Letters mailed per inhabitant

	1965	1973
Japan	97	121
US	375	414 (1972)
England	157	207
Fed. Rep. of Germany	157	168
France	156	225

Information Equipment

Density of telephone equipment per 100 inhabitants

	1970	1977
US	58.3	74.4
Japan	21.9	42.4
Mexico	3.1	5.9
Kenya	0.7	1.0

Infrastructural Investments

Informatics expenditures as % of Gross National Product

	US	US	Fed. Rep. of Germany	France
1970	2.11	1.55	1.34	1.18
1975	3.20	2.83	2.45	2.65
1980	5.50	4.75	4.60	4.40

Information Industry Revenues

US Information Corporations Revenues in US$ billion

	1970	1975
Telephone	18.2	31.3
Cable tv	0.3	0.7
Computer software & services	1.5	3.6
Newspapers/wire services	7.0	9.7
Postal service	6.3	10.0
Book publishing	3.4	4.9

The international dimension

The information age does not only affect individual countries, it has also an impact on international developments. Some figures can illustrate this international significance. In 1980 the world market for telecommunication services totalled US$ 40.2 billion. For telecommunication equipment this was approximately the same. The largest dp manufacturers in the world received some US$ 60 billion in revenues. To this should be added that part of the world market for services that is primarily linked to information and that can be estimated in 1980 to have yielded some US$ 150 billion. Adding also sales from such sectors as electronic components and consumer electronics, the 1980 world information market can be estimated at some US$ 350 billion or some 18% of total world trade.

Entering the information age

It seems a realistic projection to expect that over the next decade an increasing number of countries will enter the information age. This raises the question as to which developments determine that a country moves along the continuum from less to more (and even predominantly) information handling? The following can be offered as a partial explanation.

Size

Social processes become more complex when growing numbers of people are involved. Increased size demands coordination to avoid chaos. Coordination implies the transmission of information.

Each person added to a social organization brings a host of new data that need to be translated into functional information.

Also, more people will have more requests for information, and particularly in the 'welfare society'. This demands the expansion of various public information services.

Speed

Social complexity is further increased when the speed at which social processes unfold goes up. The growing pace at which, for example, technical innovations are introduced, demands expanding flows of information to deal with them.

It is a rather common observation that higher speeds in air or road traffic, for example, necessitate a rapid and reliable information traffic to keep accidents at a minimum.

Knowledge

Adding to social complexity is also the exponential growth of knowledge. An OECD study forecasted in 1973 that scientific/technical knowledge would increase annually by 12.5% and would reach by 1985–1987 a volume of 120–150 million documents.[13] Each day some twenty million words are added to the world's scientific and technical production. Every year twenty thousand new documents are produced in the field of economics. Between 1960 and 1975 the number of abstracts produced by Chemical Abstracts Service increased at an annual average of more than 8%. These tremendous increases in knowledge demand expanded capacities for the processing, storing and transmitting of information.

Complexity

As social systems, due to size, speed and growth of knowledge, become more complex, they need more coordination and overseeing, and by consequence their information-handling index goes up. There will be more supply of and demand for information, more people will be involved in information handling, more information equipment will be needed, and with growing complexity the equipment will have to perform ever more sophisticated functions, and lastly, more investments for information infrastructures will be needed.

Expanding industries

The international expansion of industrial production has brought about an expansion in related services, such as travel, finance, marketing and advertising, which are often highly information-intensive.

Also, during the 1970s many of the major industrial corporations became heavily involved with information through the setting up of their own media systems. One observation states that by the end of the 1970s "some three hundred United States firms whose principal business is outside of the media have developed a major video capacity for in-house corporate newscasts – some with film, videotape, and computerized editing facilities that rival those of the national networks."[14] Responding to the emerging wave of questions directed at the legitimacy of modern corporate business, the latest technical possibilities are being used in order to "tell our story more effectively than ever before."[15]

Expanding private expenditures

Increases in the private consumption of industrially manufactured goods have expanded a variety of services that are very information-intensive. The credit card business, for example, has become a major information handler. As American Express representatives state, "Our company depends on international communications and information flows for credit and authorizations, and financial transfers."[16]

Increasing affluence also leads to more expenditure in and demand for information-linked activities, such as hotel and airline reservations, entertainment, and consumer electronics. Additionally, people will also ask for more and better educational facilities, which again involves more information handling.

Services

Over the past decades productivity in agriculture and industry did turn out to be no longer sufficient to sustain economic growth. Therefore, productivity had to be increased in the services sector of the economy as a possible remedy.

And indeed the services sector has in most advanced countries become more and more important. Actually, as Daniel Bell observed, "a post-industrial society is based on services."[17]

This observation is corroborated by empirical findings in West Europe and the US. By 1978 in the countries of the European Communities some 50%

of the labour force was employed in services. And in 1980 even 70% of the US labour force was working in the services sector and contributing some 65% to the Gross National Product.[18]

With the expansion of the services sector, information handling grows since many activities in this sector are information-intensive. Examples include data processing and computer software services, banking, professional and technical advisory services, accounting, motion pictures, advertising, insurance and transportation.

Information age and information technology

For a country entering the information age it is not 'information' *per se* that is the crucial factor.

One could convincingly argue that information has always been an essential component of social processes. Therefore, the concept was broadened to 'information handling' and it is the volume, capacity and level of information handling that locates a country on the information age continuum.

However, information has been handled since the dawn of mankind's history and the generating, processing, storing and transmitting of information is not a particularly new phenomenon. But throughout history information handling was faced with severe limitations on volume, speed, range and reliability. Only recently, innovations in the technology of information handling have overcome these limitations. These innovations have facilitated the emergence of an adequate infrastructure for information handling which is the prerequisite for entering the information age. The information age needs, alongside the networks through which people, goods and energy are transported, the capacity to transport information in digital form. The response to this need has come from the convergence of the two technologies that are described in the next chapter.

Notes Chapter 1

1 This is generally related to the observation that in such countries as Mexico, Taiwan, Brazil and Korea the services sector of the economy provides an increasing contribution to the Gross National Product, even outweighing the combined contribution of agriculture and industry. See C. J. Hamelink, *Finance and Information,* Norwood: Ablex Publishing, 1983, p 4.

2 Bell proposed the concept of the post-industrial society originally in 1962 in an unpublished paper.

3 D. Bell, *The Coming of Post-Industrial Society,* New York: Basic Books, 1976 edition, p xiii.

4 M. U. Porat, *The Information Economy: Definition and Measurement,* Washington DC, US Department of Commerce/Office of Telecommunications, 1977.

5 In a more general way Porat's study claims that some 46% of the Gross National Product comes from all information activities, and that 53% of the labour income stems from informational jobs.

6 M. U. Porat, *op. cit.,* p 1.

7 S. Nora and A. Minc, *L'informatisation de la société,* Paris: La Documentation Française, 1978.

8 S. Nora and A. Minc, *op. cit.,* p 11.

9 The concept 'information age' offers a partial description only and is not meant to fully encompass today's and tomorrow's reality. This follows D. Bell's insight that 'Each conceptual scheme is a prism which selects some features, rather than others, in order to highlight historical change or, more specifically, to answer certain questions'. D. Bell, *op. cit.,* p x.

10 N. Okada, 'Some Aspects of Japan as an Information Society', in A. S. Edelstein, J. E. Bowes and S. M. Harsel (eds), *Information Societies: Comparing the Japanese and American Experiences,* Seattle, International Communication Centre, School of Communications, University of Washington, 1978, p 153.

11 The results showed a considerable lag between Japan and the US. If the Japanese index score was in 1965 set at 100, the US scored 242. By 1973 the Japanese score had gone up to 221, and the US score to 531. *Cf.* A. S. Edelstein *et al, op. cit.,* p 197.

12 The Composite Information-Handling Index will be applied in forthcoming research by the Institute of Social Studies on 'The Third World and the Information Age'.

13 G. Anderla, *Information in 1985,* Paris, OECD, 1973, p 89.

14 S. Horwitz, 'On the Road to Wired City', in *Harvard Magazine,* September/October 1979, pp 18–19. Quoted in H. I. Schiller, *Who Knows: Information in the Age of the Fortune 500,* Norwood: Ablex Publishing, 1981, p 88.

15 The quote is from L. H. Warner, chairman of General Telephone & Electronics. In H. I. Schiller, *op. cit.,* p 79.

16 H. L. Freeman and J. E. Spiro, 'Services are the Major Issue of the 1980s', in *Transnational Data Report,* Vol IV No 7, 1981, p 45.

17 D. Bell, *op. cit.,* p 127.

18 H. L. Freeman and J. E. Spiro, *op. cit.,* p 45.

2 Telematics

Telecommunication and informatics

The increase in volume and complexity of information demands appropriate techniques for transmission and processing. Telecommunication technology and electronic data processing have responded to this demand and have in fact become the key instruments for information management in the information age.

Initially, these two technologies have been explored and applied in distinct ways.

For almost 80 years telecommunication technology generated and upgraded techniques for transmissions between people-centred 'transducers', such as telephones, facsimile machines and tv systems. In its development it added to transmission and transducers the technique of switching which made networking possible. When electronic data processing became available it was applied to telecommunications for the enhancement of its efficiency, particularly in switching systems.

In the course of the 1950s the two technologies became integrated: machine-centred transducers were linked with each other and with people. Computer-communication networks were created that consist of computers with communication channels attached to them that link the computers to other computers or to terminals. The networks were constructed as centralized systems in which data are transported for processing, storing or forwarding to central computers. They were also constructed as distributed systems with data traffic between decentralized computers or terminals.

Transmission through such networks commenced with the first circuits for defence systems and airline reservations. During the 1960s and 1970s they were increasingly applied also for international banking, credit control, data banks and data bases, and intergovernmental cooperation.

Presently it is not certain how much of the transnational data traffic is carried by such material-support media as discs, tapes and cards. A report to the European Community observed in 1979 that the majority of transnational data flows was still on such media.[1]

It seems a fair expectation, however, that with increasing volumes of business information traffic, telecommunication circuits (non-material-support media) will be used more and more.[2]

The widening application of computer-communication networks has been made possible by a number of technological developments which have considerably increased the performance capacity, the accessibility and the compatibility of computing and telecommunication facilities. The traditional telephone networks have greatly enlarged their capacity for data traffic through such techniques as modems and multiplexors. Modems are devices that basically perform modulation and demodulation functions. This means that they modulate the digital signal of the computer at the transmission end into the analogue signal that conventional telephone lines transport and at the receiving end they demodulate the analogue signal again into a digital signal. In large networks modems become the essential components in traffic control. As control centres they assume a range of complex performances (such as encryption and conversion) that go far beyond mere modulation and demodulation functions.

Multiplexors are devices that facilitate the transmission of two or more messages simultaneously over a single transmission line. For the expansion of networks they are important since they permit the clustering of data flows for transmission through common record carriers.

The development of optical fibres has further increased the data transmission capacity of the telephone network. They make it possible to transport digital signals through light over glass-fibre cables. An 8 mm optical fibre cable has about the same capacity as a 20 cm copper cable (some 30,000 telephone calls) and is more resistant to conditions that cause disturbances in traffic through the copper cable. Optical-fibre cables are estimated to achieve transmission speeds of some 64,000 bits per second. If an optical-fibre connection carries at a given moment 1,000 telephone calls, the cable transports per second $1,000 \times 64,000 = 64$ million bits.

A vital technological development has also been packet-switching.[3] This technique brought the telecommunications facility to a level of comparable efficiency with the data processing facility. In 1975 the Advanced Research Projects Agency of the US Department of Defence initiated the transmission of data among disparate, remote computers and terminals through a network of over 50 packet-switches based on minicomputers.[4]

An important development has also been the introduction of a non-terrestrial mode of data traffic through communication satellites. Transnational commercial satellite transmission began in 1965, when the International Telecommunications Satellite Organisation (INTELSAT) launched its first satellite 'the Early Bird' on April 6. 'Early Bird' or INTELSAT I became operational from June 28, 1965. This satellite had a capacity of 240 two-way audio-circuits or one tv channel. Three years later in 1968 a series of INTELSAT II satellites became operational with each having a capacity of 1,500 two-way audio-circuits or four tv channels. With the INTELSAT IV series the capacity became, between 1971 and 1975, 3,750 circuits plus two tv channels.

In September 1975 the first satellite of the INTELSAT IV-A series was launched with a capacity of 6,250 circuits plus two tv channels. On December 6, 1980 the first satellite of the most recent series, INTELSAT V, was launched. In this series 12 satellites with a capacity of 12,000 circuits plus two tv channels have been ordered from a consortium led by Ford Aerospace and Communications Corporation.[5] The INTELSAT VI series of satellites with 40,000 circuits is due by 1986. This capacity would correspond with projected increases in the number of telephone circuits requested by 1986. Present prognoses already indicate an increase from 22,402 circuits in 1980 to 35,046 in 1983.[6]

INTELSAT offers its member states (106 countries as at April 1981) a telecommunications network for commercial use that today accounts for over 60% of transatlantic communications.[7] An important feature of the INTELSAT operation is that over the past years the increase in capacity has been accompanied by a decrease in costs for the users (see Table IV).

On the planned INTELSAT VI series the telephone circuits can alternatively be used for voice and data transmissions. Also groups of telephone circuits can be utilized for wideband data transmissions.[8] With the application of Time Division Multiple Access (TDMA) techniques in the new satellites they will become both technically and economically better suited for the handling of digital data traffic.

Data networks have also become more attractive through the developments in computer hardware and software. Micro-electronics, which since the early 1970s has produced the microprocessor, made it possible to apply computer capacity very broadly and cheaply.[9] As a matter of fact, small computers have become vital to data communication networks, both in the communications and the processing facilities.

Particularly important are the so-called intelligent network processors that function as interfaces between the mainframe data-processing equipment and the data network. Network processors have a variety of tasks, among which

Table IV INTELSAT 1965–1980

Year	No Satellites	Voice Circuits	TV channels	Charges	
				Telephone Circuit	**TV channel**
1965	1	240	1	$64.000 p/year	$14,80 p/min
1980	12	25.500	10	$10.800 p/year	$ 8,00 p/min

are the control of network connections, the checking of errors, editing of messages and regulating of flows and queues of messages.

Important for data networks have also been innovations in network architecture. A data network consists of computers (the 'nodes' of the network) that perform each specific sub-task (processing functions), and between them information is exchanged through the communications facility. The network architecture regulates the complex interactions among the distributed functions of the network.

Together with these developments in hardware there have been considerable advances in the accompanying software and peripheral equipment. New programming languages were developed in order to improve the machine-user relationship and to design a mode of instructing the machine that would be close to the user's language.

Since computers can only perform the functions they are expected to carry out for the solving of problems if they are adequately instructed through programmes, the development of software has been an essential component of computer development.

With the increasing speed of performance of the computer, also the speed of the peripheral equipment had to be improved. Input and output devices had to be developed that matched the performance of the central processing unit of the computer.

Developments in hardware, software and peripheral equipment have largely contributed to the rapid growth of the utilization of computers. This growth is documented in Table V.

The technological developments described so far have contributed to the convergence of telecommunication and data processing into 'telematics'.[10]

'Telematics' implies that the communication and processing functions that used to be performed by distinct systems can now be operated by one

Table V Number of Computers in the World

	1960	1970	1973	1978	1983	1988
US	5,500	65,000	110,000	200,000	400,000	700,000
West Europe	1,500	21,000	55,000	110,000	225,000	450,000
Japan	400	6,000	19,000	45,000	70,000	140,000
Other countries	1,600	18,000	46,000	95,000	205,000	460,000
Total	9,000	110,000	230,000	450,000	900,000	1,750,000

Source: Diebold Europe, 1979.

integrated system. This system facilitates a significant increase in volume, rapidity, reliability and complexity of data-handling. The capacity of this system will be further enlarged with the growing sophistication of computers, computing and telecommunication carriers. In this respect particularly decisive are: integrated circuit technology, computer programming, satellite technology and optical fibre technology.

Remote resource sensing

An important application of 'telematics' is the collection from outer space of data about natural resources, the transmission and the processing of such data.

Since 1972 remote resource sensing is mainly done by NASA's Landsat satellites. The NASA programme has expanded considerably over the past years, due to developments in sensoring and processing technologies and greater interest for the 'sensed data' on the part of governmental and industrial users.

Remote resource sensing has been applied to explore iron formations, to measure sugar cane and rice crop, to map river sediments and forests, to oceanography and to demographic mapping. Since 1972, for example, over one billion dollars in oil reserves and several millions of dollars worth of mineral reserves have been located. The real problem with remote sensing is to extract useful information from data the sensors collect. This demands the application of very sophisticated image-processing equipment and related software. A few large corporations offer such data processing services: Earth Satellite Corporation, IBM and General Electric. An important vendor of Landsat imagery is the Earth Resources Observation Systems (EROS) of the

US Department of the Interior. In 1980 its data were for 57% sold to US customers and for 43% to non-US clients, among which were the USSR and China.

Table VI Distribution US Customers for EROS Imagery in 1980

	in %
Industry	31
Government	39
University	17
Individuals	13

Source: Constructed from documentation by the US Department of the Interior, Geological Survey, EROS Data Centre.

The telematics market

The world market for telematics technology is concentrated in the hands of few transnational corporations. Illustrative are data processing, electronic components and telecommunication.

Data processing

The international computer market is largely dominated by the products of American firms, manufactured either in the US or by these firms' foreign subsidiaries.

In 1979 one corporation, IBM, garnered 50% of the international data processing market with revenues from computer products and services exceeding US$ 18 billion. In the same year US corporations accounted for 81% of the world computer market, Japanese corporations 7%, French corporations 3.5%, and West German corporations 2.8%.

In 1979 out of all the computers installed worldwide 78% came from US manufacturers.

Projections for 1984 estimate the total world market for computer products at some US$ 110 billion. The 15 largest corporations are expected to have

Table VII Projected 1982 Revenues for Data Processing Corporations
(in US$ millions)

Rank	Corporation	Country	Revenues
1	IBM	US	35,200
2	Digital Equipment	US	6,400
3	Control Data	US	5,000
4	Hewlett Packard	US	4,500
5	Sperry Univac	US	4,400
6	NCR	US	4,300
7	Burroughs	US	3,500
8	Honeywell	US	2,700
9	CII-Honeywell-Bull	France	2,600
10	Olivetti	Italy	2,400
11	ICL	UK	2,300
12	Fujitsu	Japan	2,200
13	Nippon Electric	Japan	2,200
14	Nixdorf	W Germany	1,800
15	Hitachi	Japan	1,700

Source: Martin Simpson & Co., New York, 1981.

revenues of US$ 81 billion (which is 74%) and IBM is expected to total over US$ 35 billion, which amounts to 32% of the world market, and 43% of the 15 leading corporations (see Table VII).

Although Japan's share in the world market is definitely on the increase, various publications of the Japanese Ministry of Trade and Industry (MITI) warn against being over-optimistic about its capacity to catch up with US data processing technology. With its high productivity, sophisticated infrastructure for the adaptation of imported technology and its protectionist trading policies, Japan has strong competitive power, but there is a lack of real innovative research which could turn out to be a serious obstacle, particularly in the field of software development where Japan is certainly lagging behind. The Japanese Government is, however, determined to make a bid for world leadership in data processing and for the next decade plans to spend US$ 300 million on research and development, particularly for the 'super computer' (the fastest and most powerful system designed so far) and for the fifth-generation computer. US trade analysts expect an 8.3% share of the world data processing market for Japan by 1985.

For many years data processing products and prices have been defined by IBM control of the industry, leaving only little space for other contenders and hardly any space for new entrants. In 1980 IBM obtained US$ 21.3 billion revenues out of US$ 55.6 billion for the top 100 US data processing corporations. The strength of IBM has made it possible for this firm to become vertically integrated in a strict sense, i.e. manufacturing the whole range of products within the data processing field. IBM now produces, alongside its large general-purpose computers, also the small business systems machines and its own electronic components. As a matter of fact, IBM is the only large computer manufacturer that produces all the components it needs for its computers.[11]

Electronic components

With the advent of integrated circuit technology (the possibility to incorporate increasing numbers of electronic components on such semiconductors as silicium, germanium and gallium arsenide), the manufacturers of electronic components became strongly involved with the data processing industry. The leaders in the manufacturing of discrete components, such as diodes and transistors, (Texas Instruments, Motorola, Fairchild) became also central to the production of integrated circuits. In 1978 the world market for integrated circuits reached approximately US$ 4.25 billion. US corporations, Texas Instruments, Motorola, Fairchild, INTEL, Advanced Micro Devices, and National Semiconductor, accounted for 70% and total US production for 80%. Japanese manufacturers took another 15% of the world market.

In 1979 the eight largest producers totalled revenues of some US$ 3.6 billion. Texas Instruments, Motorola, and INTEL realized 50% of this total (see Table VIII). The US firms are undoubtedly leading, but the Japanese integrated circuit industry is growing fast. From US$ 132 million revenues in 1976, it reached over the two billion mark by 1980.

European corporations are still largely dependent upon the US for advanced integrated circuit technology. In 1979 West Europe used US$ 1.6 billion worth of integrated circuits and produced only US$ 500 million worth (see Table IX).

Within the integrated circuit industry the fastest growing sector is the manufacturing of microprocessors. In 1979 the top ten in world microprocessor production were Texas Instruments, Philips, Motorola, Fairchild, National Semiconductor, INTEL, ITT, Mostek, Siemens, and AEG/Telefunken. The leader of the industry, Texas Instruments, controlled some 17% of the world market.[12]

Table VIII Revenues Largest Integrated Circuit Producers in 1979
(in US$ millions)

Rank	Corporation	Country	Revenues
1	Texas Instruments	US	925
2	National Semiconductor	US	515
3	Motorola	US	500
4	INTEL	US	430
5	Nippon Electric	Japan	430
6	Fairchild	US	330
7	Signetics	US	280
8	Hitachi	Japan	250

Source: Ministère de l'Industrie, France, 1980.

Table IX Shares West European Integrated Circuit Market in 1979

Rank	Corporation	Country	Market Share
1	Texas Instruments	US	15.9%
2	Philips	Netherlands	14.7%
3	INTEL	US	8.0%
4	Motorola	US	8.0%
5	Siemens	W Germany	7.5%
6	National Semiconductor	US	4.7%
7	ITT	US	4.2%
8	Nippon Electric	Japan	3.1%

Source: Mackintosh Consultants, 1981.

Telecommunication

In 1978, 13 telecommunication manufacturers dominated 90% of the world market for telecommunication equipment.

Out of an estimated world market of US$ 34 billion in 1978 three US corporations (Western Electric, ITT, and GT&E) accounted for over 52% (see Table X).

Also in the development and application of satellite technology concentration is the major characteristic. In terms of R&D contracts, numbers of launching vehicles and spacecraft manufactured, support systems designed, produced and serviced, actual operational facilities maintained, present data suggest that some eight corporations control 50% of the world market. These are: TRW, McDonnell Douglas, Ford Aerospace & Communications, Hughes Aircraft, General Electric, IBM, Comsat, and RCA.

The market for modems is presently for some 25% controlled by AT&T and is estimated to reach US$ 150 million by 1983. In 1978 the market for multiplexors reached US$ 375 million with AT&T accounting for some 20%. This market is expected to grow to US$ 750 million by 1983. The largest manufacturers after AT&T are Timeplex, Codex, Infotron, and General Datacom. Leading the market for optical fibres, which is growing from US$ 20 million in 1976 to US$ 1 billion by 1987, are AT&T, ITT, and Siemens.[13]

Table X World Market Shares Telecommunication Manufacturers in 1978

Rank	Corporation	Country	Market Share
1	Western Electric	US	23%
2	ITT	US	15.3%
3	GT & E	US	14%
4	Siemens	W Germany	8.3%
5	Hitachi	Japan	5.6%
6	Ericsson	Sweden	4.7%
7	Northern-Telecom	Canada	4.2%
8	Thomson-CSF	France	3.8%
9	CGE	France	2.5%
10	Philips	Netherlands	2.5%
11	General Electric	UK	2.0%
12	Nippon Electric	Japan	2.0%
13	Plessey	UK	1.3%

Source: Arthur D. Little, 1980.

Notes Chapter 2

1 Interim report of the Joint Report on Data Security and Confidentiality, April 1979, p 4. This report was prepared by the Gesellschaft für Mathematik und Datenverarbeitung (FRG), l'Institut de Recherche d'Informatique et d'Automatique (France), and the National Computing Centre (UK).

2 – Trade journal *Computerworld* (January 5, 1978) estimated the US business communications market to grow from $14 billion in 1965 to $31 million in 1974. It expected this market to reach $61 billion in 1980 and total more than $100 billion by 1985.

   – The Harris Corporation expects that US firms will spend more than $300 million on equipment for private satellite networks up till 1985 (from *Transnational Data Report*, Vol II No 8, March 1980, p 12).

3 Packet-switching is a technique that makes it possible to dissect information flows into segments ('packets'), to link addresses and other information to the packets, and to guide the packets through multiple independent channels from their source to their destination.

4 The network was called ARPANET.

5 Other participants in the consortium are Thomson-CSF (France), GEC-Marconi (UK), Messerschmitt-Bolköw-Blohm (FRG), Mitsubishi (Japan), and Selenia (Italy). The INTELSAT satellites cost US$ 34 million each. Launching costs (by the Atlas-Centaur rocket) are another US$ 42 million per satellite. The planned INTELSAT VI series is expected to cost more than US$ 1 billion.

6 Source: C. Titulaer, *Televisiesatellieten*, Rotterdam: Wyt, 1980, p 29.

7 Part of transatlantic communications still uses undersea cables. In 1983 a new transatlantic cable is expected to be finished. This will be the TAT-7 with a capacity of 4,000 telephone circuits.

8 For wideband data transmissions INTELSAT capacity reaches up to 1.5 megabits per second.

9 By the end of 1971 the firm INTEL announced the production of the microprocessor: the central processing unit (CPU) of the computer printed on a tiny wafer of silicium – the silicon chip.

10 Telematics comes from the French 'telematique'. Also used is the concept 'compunications' – this was coined by the Harvard University Programme on Information Resource Policy.

11 Sources for data processing markets:
   Datamation, March 1978, July 1980, and January 1981; *L'Industrie informatique dans le monde*, DAFSA, Paris, 1976; Arthur D. Little, 1980, and Martin Simpson & Co., 1981; Ministère de l'Industrie, *Les chiffres clés de l'informatisation*, Paris: La Documentation Française, 1980.

12 Sources for electronic components markets:
   Ministère de l'Industrie, o.c.; OECD, *Impact of multinational enterprises on national scientific and technical capacities*, OECD Directorate for Science, Technology and Industry, Paris, December 1977.

13 Sources for telecommunication markets:
   Ministère de l'Industrie, o.c.; *Datamation*, June 1980; C. J. Hamelink, Imperialism in satellite technology', *WACC Journal*, Vol xxvi No 1, 1979.

3 Data Networks and Data Flows

Public or private institutions involved with data traffic may have a number of reasons for developing or joining computer communication networks.

- Direct financial benefits might accrue from the sharing of expensive communication facilities with more users in different locations. An airline alone could not afford to maintain a worldwide reservation system; as a joint network between many airlines it is possible.
- Such benefits might also accrue from the sharing of access to information that would otherwise be very expensive to use.
- Benefits might also accrue from the possibility to transport and process large volumes of data in a fast and reliable manner for improved management, marketing and productivity.
- Networks can meet the need for centralized information management in order to monitor fluctuating exchange rates and commodity prices.
- Networks can reduce inventory costs by improving the flow of materials between the units of the corporation.
- Benefits might accrue from the possibility to share otherwise dispersed resources.[1]
- Institutions might have activities that are by definition geared towards international communications, such as is the case with Interpol or the World Health Organisation.

A number of network types can be distinguished. A basic division can be made into public and private networks.

Public networks

These networks are initiated and regulated by public authorities that enable subscribers to communicate with each other. The network is only involved with the transport of data.

By the end of the 1970s in West Europe the French PTT had initiated the TRANSPAC network, the Spanish National Telephone Company had introduced CTNE, and the British Post Office experimented with the Experimental Packet-Switching System (EPSS). In Canada there were the networks INFOSWITCH and DATAPAC and in Japan Nippon Telephone & Telegraph Corporation developed the DDX network. The largest public data network is presently EURONET, initiated by the Commission of the European Communities and operative as a data transmission infrastructure since 1980. The establishment of EURONET did cost some US$ 20 million. Its chief objective is to provide a public on-line network for scientific/technical data bases. Through switching centres in London, Frankfurt, Paris and Rome some 130 data bases are accessible since 1981. An organisation called DIANE (Direct Information Access Network) is assigned to contract data bases for the network. Present data bases are offered by 23 data producers and contain some 40 million bibliographic references in medicine, agriculture, chemistry and aerospace.

Private networks

In a study for the OECD it was estimated that Europe counted in the late 1970s some 150 data networks, of which 120 were private networks.[2]

They are mainly initiated and used by private corporations for the transport and processing of data pertinent to their commercial and financial operations.

Examples include IBM's private network Retain with data banks in the US and the UK. The network is accessible to IBM engineers through terminals all over the world. It provides in particular updated technical details on disfunctions of computer systems.

Digital Equipment Corporation has its network for maintenance services. The European maintenance centre in Valbonne can be accessed through terminals for diagnoses. A good illustration is provided also by the private data network of electronics manufacturer Motorola Inc. The network gives access to the programmes and data bases of two computer centres (Illinois and Arizona, US) from Motorola locations around the world. The data network uses 26 dedicated circuits throughout the world; 102 high-speed printers and 4,000 interactive terminals are hooked up with the network. Daily, over one billion characters flow through the network. It is used for engineering design, inventory control, production schedules, sales data, product test parameters, invoices and a variety of time-sharing computer applications.[3]

A further distinction between data networks could be made on the basis of the services they provide. This would distinguish between record-carriers, value-added networks, computer service companies and closed user groups.

Record-carriers

They provide the communication infrastructure for users of transnational computer traffic. They facilitate data transmission from points of collection to points of storage and to points of usage. They use as communication facilities undersea cables or communication satellites. The largest international record carriers are RCA Global Communications Inc., ITT World Communications Inc., Western Union International and TRT Telecommunications Corp.

The largest telecommunications firm in the world, AT&T, which established in 1956 (with the British Post Office) the first transatlantic cable, is since 1964 limited to providing voice services only. In December 1979 the Federal Communications Commission in the US revised this earlier decision to the extent that AT&T could also transport data for its customers.

Value-added networks (VANs)

VANs lease communication facilities from record-carriers, link these with computers and add services such as data storage, data processing, electronic mail, packet-switching and support services. They sell these services to their clients.

VANs offer an effective utilization of computer capacity which is attractive to the client who does not have to lease standard lines from the record-carriers and does not have to invest in expensive computer equipment.

According to a Frost & Sullivan report, the intelligent network the VANs offer "can be a very attractive approach for interactive DP operators, service bureaux, and other selected users who need access to a variety of host computers and data bases." Data communication users express increasing interest in using VANs, and in 1980 they formed already a US$ 500 million market.[4]

The largest private transnational VANs are Tymnet and Telenet. Tymnet is operational since 1971 as a wholly owned subsidiary of Tymshare. Since 1980 the network is accessible from 36 countries. Telenet was founded in 1972 by Bolt, Beranek and Newman Inc., and became operational in 1975. For its international services Telenet uses the facilities of RCA, ITT and TRT. The largest markets for Telenet's international service are computer service bureaux, data base firms, and transnational corporations.

Telenet is presently owned by one of the largest US utility corporations, General Telephone & Electronics.

Computer service companies

They offer through the facilities of the VANs or their own networks computer hardware and software to their users. They may combine this with access to large data banks and data bases. Thus, they facilitate time-shared data processing and data base retrieval services.

Many organizations find it cheaper to rely on service bureaux than to build up and maintain their own computer and telecommunication infrastructures.

Among the largest service companies are General Electric and Tymshare (see Table XI).

Tymshare offers its clients a host of services such as assistance in corporate planning, accounting, marketing, sales management, production control and administration. Among these clients are more than 1,000 banks.

The Mark III network through which General Electric offers its services was in 1970 the first to offer international time-sharing services. Like Tymshare, it has many banks among its clients.

Table XI Ten Largest US Computer-service Companies
(1979 sales in US$ millions)

Computer Sciences	416.1
Automatic Data Processing	400.8
General Electric	350.0
Electronic Data Systems	311.5
McDonnell Douglas	252.0
Tymshare	176.0
System Development	163.1
United Telecom	138.4
Bradford National	120.1
Planning Research	119.6

Source: Datamation, July 1980.

Closed user group networks

These are initiated by a specific group of users that need them to deliver services geared to their operations. Most important examples are the international airlines (with the SITA system) and the international banks (with the S.W.I.F.T. system).

Flows

The different types of data flowing through the present computer communication networks can tentatively be classified as follows:

Intra-company flows

These are mainly flows of data between company's subsidiaries and headquarters (where they are processed). They may pertain to production, inventory, management, financing, personnel or research and development.

Inter-company flows

These are mainly flows of transaction data, i.e. data that relate to transactions, such as commodity trade, funds transfers or reservations. They flow between network users in different locations.

Data bank/data base flows

Flows that transport data for information retrieval. These flows can go through public and private networks.

Service flows

These are flows that transport data for the remote performance of computer services.

Intergovernmental flows

Mainly flows of data pertaining to the military, criminal offence and scientific/technical (meteorology, agriculture, health care, etc.) subjects.

Growth of transnational data flows

As indicated before, there are no exact data available that would allow calculation of the present volume of transnational data flows in its totality and according to different types of data and networks. It is also not possible to present clear empirical evidence about past developments and future trends based upon such data. However, using different sources and measures – that are not always comparable – one can tentatively give some suggestions as to the growth of transnational data flows.

Some indications come from the responses given by OECD countries to a questionnaire on Transborder Flows of Non-personal Data. Non-personal data are important if – indeed, as several sources seem to suggest – they form the majority of present transnational data flows.

The data from the OECD countries that participated are not comprehensive. They are often just estimates. Varying definitions and measurements make comparison difficult and in some cases impossible.

The overall impression from the study is that the flow of computer data across national borders is increasing more rapidly than the overall growth of non-voice communications.[5]

Estimates for Australia, for example, indicate for 1979 a 50% growth rate for switched data traffic and 20% for non-voice communications. It has to be observed, however, that switched data traffic is only 5% in total non-voice traffic.[6]

Growth of transnational data flows could also be constructed from increases in sales of computing services abroad, i.e. exports of computing services. The problem with these figures is that not all of them pertain to data flows; some may relate to servicing, maintenance, training and software.

In the UK between 1971 and 1977 there was a more than fivefold increase in overseas billings of the computer services industry. Again, it has to be observed here, that in 1977 overseas billings amounted only to 5.1% of total computer services billings.[7]

Growth and size of the computer services market in the US and West-European countries are shown in Table XII.

An indication of data flow growth also comes from the increasing numbers of data base searches. The number of data searches in North America and West Europe increased from 3.3 million in 1973 to 12.5 million in 1976.[8] The number of users of data base services increased between 1965 and 1978 from 10,000 to 2 million.[9]

Another measure for data flow growth would be to look at the numbers of terminals installed.

A study on West-European data communication found in 1979 a total of 625,000 terminals and projected a growth by 1987 to 3,960,000 terminals. Other growth indications from the same study are the number of NTPs (Network Terminating Points – points of connection between user equipment and PTT transmission facilities) from 393,000 in 1979 to 1,620,000 by 1987.

The total number of transactions originated during the average working day is expected to grow from 136 million to 794 million by 1987. The total number of bits during the average working day is expected to grow from 1310 billion to 9820 billion by 1987 (see Table XIII).[10]

Table XII US and West European Market for Computer Services, 1978

Country	1978 market in US$ millions	Growth percentage 1978/1979
France	1,335.8	27.9
Fed. Rep. of Germany	949.7	12.8
England	771.0	36.4
Italy	523.9	21.2
Sweden	407.0	10.9
Netherlands	404.8	22.8
Denmark	263.4	17.9
Switzerland	226.5	13.8
Belgium	204.5	17.4
Spain	170.1	31.7
Norway	158.0	17.4
Finland	146.9	22.7
Austria	100.3	13.6
Total Western Europe	5,709.0	15.8
Total US	6,765.0	12.9

Source: Science Corporation, 1980.

Yet another indication for data flow growth could be borrowed from a joint study by Arthur D. Little and AEG/Telefunken. This forecast on developments in the world telecommunications market expects that revenues from data traffic will increase with an annual 9.5% from US$ 2.9 billion in 1980 to US$ 7.3 billion by 1990.[11]

The present situation seems to be one in which transnational data traffic is still relatively minor compared to total telecommunication traffic.

There are indications of rapid growth although this cannot satisfactorily be substantiated.

Factors that may speed up or slow down the growth of transnational data flows are:

- If data flows were to be increasingly applied as a key instrument for transnational corporate management, this would be an important factor in their growth.
- Another factor stimulating growth could be if the international market for computer services were to keep expanding.
- A potential obstacle to growth could be the costs. Communication tariffs tend to become the largest portion of computer network costs. Presently, costs of private (leased) circuits are high: the average annual cost of an international circuit in West Europe is US$ 20,000. The implication of these costs is that only the largest organisations can use and benefit from transnational data networks. Developments in telecommunication technology could lead to lower costs and more intensive use of data flows. In their study for the OECD, the Logica team found that international private networks could achieve costs between 1–10 US cents per 1,000 characters transmitted; this would compare to 300 cents for telephone calls and 60 cents for the use of telex.[12]
- A potential obstacle is also current bandwidths. If one were to rapidly increase data volumes, this would demand the application of telecommunication channels that could handle this. Optical fibre is the technology that meets expanded data flow requirements. At present, however, only a minor part of telecommunication connections uses optical fibre cables.[13]
- The further development of Very Large Scale Integration will facilitate the production of intelligent terminals with advanced processing capacity which would stimulate the growth of networks with distributed data processing.
- Other technological developments might facilitate data flow growth, such as the miniaturization of computer hardware. The application of microprocessors will make computer capacity available at many more locations than before and at much lower costs.
- If technological developments were to stimulate growth, there could be obstacles posed by international and national regulations. National governments and the international community might – in weighing costs and benefits of expanded data flows – decide that the social costs are too high (or too unpredictable) and restrain growth.

**Table XIII Forecast Main Features West European
Data Communications Market**

	1979	1983	1987
Number of Network			
Terminating Points	393,000	832,000	1,620,000
Number of Terminals	625,000	1,720,000	3,960,000
Number of Transactions per			
average working day	136 million	375 million	794 million
Total number of Bits per			
average working day	1310 billion	3970 billion	9820 billion

Source: Eurodata Foundation, Eurodata '79, London.

Notes Chapter 3

1 Ford Motor Company installed its network in 1978 and claims to have saved US$ 180 million in the design of the new Escort (type Erica) through the international pooling of its best designers from different locations. Source: *Transnational Data Report,* Vol III No 6, October 1980.

2 Logica Ltd, *The Usage of International Data Networks in Europe,* Paris: OECD, 1979.

3 Source: *Transnational Data Report,* Vol IV No 7, 1981, pp 37–40.

4 Frost & Sullivan Inc., New York, quoted in *Telecommunications,* April 1981.

5 Expert Group on Transborder Data Barriers and the Protection of Privacy, Paris: OECD document: DSTI/ICCP/79.49, August 16, 1979.

6 Ibidem, p 6.

7 Ibidem, p 11.

8 Paul B. Silverman, 'International Telecommunications as a Tool for Technology Transfer', paper for Technology Exchange '78, Atlanta, February 9, 1978.

9 P. I. van Velse, 'Aspects of a European Information Industry', paper for the Commission of the European Communities, Luxembourg, September 5, 1979.

10 M. Benedetti, 'Eurodata '79: the growth of data communications in Western Europe', paper for the IBI Conference on Transborder Data Flow Policies, Rome, June 1980.

11 Source: *Media-Info,* Amsterdam: VNU, Vol I No 26, 1981, p 309.

12 Ph. Hughes and R. Sasson, 'The Development of Data Networks in Europe', paper in *ONLINE, Data Regulation: European and Third World Realities,* Uxbridge, 1978, p 23.

13 In 1978 all optical fibre connections in the world amounted to some 900 kilometers. Presently, revenues from optical fibre production are estimated to reach US$ 40 million (in 1980). The largest manufacturers (AT&T and ITT) expect that by 1985 revenues will increase tenfold. Source: G. Bylinsky, 'Fibre optics finally sees the light', *Fortune,* March 24, 1980.

4 Transnational Corporations and Transnational Data Flows

Recording the views from industry representatives, there can be little doubt that they share the observation by F. A. Bernasconi, Director General of IBI: "Transborder data flows are the life blood of transnational corporations."[1] One example to illustrate this: "As an international bank, our business is entirely dependent upon the free flow of instantaneous communication. In the course of our banking business, we need to have minute-by-minute intelligence from the money markets across the world," states Robert E. L. Walker, Vice President of Continental Illinois Bank.[2] Another banker, Rossiter W. Langhorne, formerly Vice President of Manufacturers Hanover Trust, broadens this to the whole business community, "In today's international marketplace, repetitive timely processing of business transactions is the basis for reliable service and survival of the business community. Without the present state of data processing and communications technology this could not be accomplished."[3] John L. Rankine, Director of Standards, Product Safety and Data Security for IBM, elaborates this, "We need this flow of information in order to communicate worldwide engineering design and manufacturing information as well as to inform our customers about technical changes and improvements to our products on which, in turn, their operations depend. It is also necessary for us to match available engineering, technological and marketing support with user requirements. All this inevitably requires that we maintain an inventory of the employee skills available worldwide so that we can provide people with necessary skills wherever they are needed. We must have the ability to move financial and operational information among our various organisations as freely as possible. Finally, we must interact continuously with international banking and transportation facilities, such as airlines, which, in turn, also depend on a free flow of information to conduct their operations."[4]

It will be clear that the statements quoted above do not necessarily substantiate the actual importance of data flows for the performance of international business. To prove this, more material would have to be independently collected.

Theoretically, the significance of data communication – as a fast, reliable and secure way of transmission of information's raw resources – can be deduced from the basic need of information for business. – Tentatively, four areas of information requirements can be identified:

a. Information is needed about competitor's behaviour. The complexity of this evidently increases with the degree of transnationalisation and diversification. An important part of this information relates to technological (product) development.
b. Information about the behaviour of the consumers in the market sectors where the corporation operates is also essential.
c. Then there is an obvious need for that type of scientific/technical information that relates to the specific products the corporation manufactures.
d. Lastly, there is a constant need for information about the economic, fiscal, legal and political environments in which the corporation conducts its operations.

These informational needs correlate with the external demand for the corporation to cope effectively with different and often changing environments. Also, as will be argued later, for the internal control and coordination of the corporation the access to and the use of data is an important element in effective performance.

Data and business

The use of data to conduct business is no new phenomenon. Data and their processed format (information) have always been an intrinsic part of a variety of business transactions. Data routes and trading routes have for a long time run parallel, and in 13th-century Europe merchants were already called 'custodes novellarum' (guardians of the news): they collected, transported and processed data – used them for their own activities and sold them to others.

Only recently this data-business interlock has undergone important changes.

There is a *quantitative* change in that the volume of data for the conducting of business has drastically increased, to the extent that only electronic intelligence can cope with it. This is due to the growth of international trade, of direct foreign investments and of the institutions involved in these. The rapid transnationalisation of industrial and financial business since the 1950s has created large, complex institutions with specific organisational models and strategic designs that implied new data requirements. Increasingly, the effective operation of these transnational corporations relied as much on their traditional direct productive activities as upon their capability to collect and transport data and to process them into productive information/knowledge. The structure of the transnational corporation became data-centred. By consequence a series of new activities sprang up: specialization in the collecting of data, the storing of data, the processing of data and the transmission of data. These are industrial activities that need the hardware and software supplies of a growing sector of domestic and international economies: the data processing industry.

There is also a *qualitative* change in that the role of data developed from being a vital support factor into being the essential factor. Data manipulation used to be necessary in order to execute industrial and agricultural activities; with increasing automation, data manipulation becomes the activity itself. Robots taking over from factory workers are a case in point, as is the microprocessor application in agricultural mechanization. The services sector of the economy is an even clearer illustration with such developments as the automated office, electronic mail and electronic funds transfer.

Data in business

A classification of the relationships between data flows and transnational corporations could distinguish three categories:

a. Corporations for which data are the main product line;
b. Corporations for which data are the lifeblood;
c. Corporations for which data are the key instrument for effective management.

Data as main product line

In this category fall:

Data producers

Corporations which have established data banks or data bases stocking their internal data or collecting data from outside sources.

Often the private data producers stock data that are originally generated by large public organisations, such as the OECD, IMF, World Bank, European Space Agency, or the US Department of Commerce.

Data will be stocked in an organised format in data banks or data bases. Data banks contain so-called source data (factual) and data bases contain reference data (bibliographic). In 1979 out of an identified 528 data bases, the US-owned data bases had 63% of the records stocked. A majority of these records (65%) was linked with science and technology.[5]

In the period 1970–1975 the number of data bases in the world grew strongly, but since 1978 data banks seem to have taken over. The use of data banks increases more rapidly than with data bases, and their on-line accessibility is greater.[6] The large majority of data banks is US-owned, and some 70% of information retrieval from data banks is estimated to take place in the US.[7]

One estimate puts the 1979 overall revenue for data bank use at US$ 1.5 billion with some 80% stemming from the sales of financial/economic information.[8]

Among the largest data banks for this type of information are Chase Econometrics (a subsidiary of Chase Manhattan Bank) and Data Resources Inc. They share a considerable portion of the world market for financial/economic data: Chase Econometrics 20% and Data Resources Inc., 60%.[9]

Data vendors

Corporations which distribute data by providing on-line access to data producers or by publishing data base products.

Very large data vendors are Lockheed Information Systems, Systems Development Corporation and Bibliographic Retrieval Services Inc. All three are US-owned. Lockheed provides through its DIALOG retrieval system access to 87 on-line interactive data bases (see Table XIV). Systems Development Corporation and Bibliographical Retrieval Services provide access to 54 and 18 data bases, respectively.

Using data bases as a source, a variety of products is published in printed and electronic formats. In 1981 total data base publishing in the US was estimated to reach the US$ 2 billion mark.

On-line data base publishing with revenues of some US$ 450 million in 1980 (for the US) is expected to have an annual growth rate of 25%.[10] The largest data base publishers are McGraw Hill, Dun & Bradstreet, American Express and CBS.

Data network providers

Corporations which provide access to the products of the data vendors.

Several corporations have created time-sharing networks to provide users with on-line access to huge volumes of data and to the related software for the manipulation of the data. Such services have become international business over recent years through the activities of the value-added networks, such as Telenet and Tymnet. Tymnet, for example, is the distributor for Data Resources Inc.

Table XIV Lockheed Information Systems

Illustration of data bases to which Lockheed offers on-line access, 1978

Name Data Base	Subject
AIM/ARM	Abstracts of instructional and research materials in vocational and technical education
Art bibliographies Modern	Publications in modern art and design from 1800 onwards
Chemical Abstracts	Bibliographical data and keyword phrases for chemistry and chemical engineering
Defence Market Measures System	US Defence Dept. contract awards
Environment Abstracts	Environmental literature
ERIC	Research and journals in education
International Statistical Abstracts	230,000 published forecasts
Metals Abstracts	Worldwide metallurgical literature
Science Citation Index	Multidisciplinary index to science and technology literature

Source: Bulletin of the American Society for Information Science, Vol 4 No 6, 1978.

Data service providers

Corporations that offer computer services associated with data processing. They facilitate the use of hardware and software and provide support services such as training, leasing, maintenance and systems protection. Service companies are a heterogeneous group that, besides a few major firms, comprises a multitude of small firms that offer highly dedicated services, often on a limited geographical basis. Three main categories of service companies can be distinguished:

a. The main frame manufacturers: they are interested in binding clients to their equipment. Examples include General Electric (offering services through Mark III) and Control Data Corporation (offering services through Cybernet).
b. The large computer users: they are interested in finding full employment for their equipment. An example is Boeing Co., with its Boeing Computer Service Company.
c. The independent service companies: they have specialized in this field. An example is Tymshare, a service company using the network of its subsidiary Tymnet.

The market for computer services is growing rapidly (some 20% annually) and the provision of such services is by the end of the century expected to be among the largest industries in the US.[11]

According to INPUT (the London-based market research firm for the data processing industry), the US revenues for overall computer services will increase from US$ 14.2 billion in 1980 to US$ 28.9 billion in 1984. Leaving out software products, turnkey systems and professional services, for processing services only the West-European market is estimated to grow from US$ 4.2 billion in 1980 to US$ 8.7 billion in 1984, and the US market from US$ 8.4 billion in 1980 to US$ 18.8 billion in 1985.[12]

Data carriers

Corporations that provide the basic transmission facility for data flows. The largest data carriers are US-owned corporations. They are the international record-carriers, RCA Global Communications Inc., ITT World Communications Inc., Western Union International, TRT Telecommunications Corp., and FTC Communications (Table XV). The major portion of their revenues stems from international telex services, but they are all preparing to provide increasingly sophisticated digital data services over the coming years. They offer lease channels for voice/data services, integration of networks for various communication functions, and enable the US-based VANs to connect with foreign public data networks, They have to use the cable or satellite facilities of three telecommunication monopolies, AT&T, Western Union Telco, and Comsat (Table XVI).

Table XV US International Record-Carriers, 1979
(operating revenues in US$ millions)

RCA Global Communications Inc.	181
ITT World Communications Inc.	170
Western Union International	112
TRT Telecommunications Corp.	28
FTC Communications	5

Source: Federal Communications Commission, Statistics of Communications Common Carriers, 1975–1979, Washington: FCC, 1979.

Table XVI Revenues Data Communications, 1979
(in US$ millions)

AT&T	2,309
Western Union Corp.	451.2
Comsat	16.2

Source: Datamation, August 1980.

Data communication manufacturers

Although they are not directly involved necessarily with data as such, these corporations can consider data a main product line since they manufacture the essential hardware for data flows.

This group of corporations includes such mainframe manufacturers as IBM, NCR, Burroughs and Control Data, but also several independent data communication vendors. The product range in the group comprises computer front-ends, network controllers, modems, multiplexors and test equipment. For 1979 sales of front-ends and modems/multiplexors see Table XVII.

In 1979 installed front-ends, modems and multiplexors in the US had a monetary value of US$ 3 billion. The projected annual growth for these products was 21%. For computer front-ends alone the US market was in 1979 US$ 1.4 billion, and IBM accounted for 55%.

One estimate says that the overall market for all data transmission equipment could reach US$ 65 billion by 1987.[13]

Data as lifeblood

In this category fall the corporations whose operations require by necessity international communication, such as airlines, banks, credit bureaux, investment advisers, or hotel chains. These corporations transport and process data that are directly related to their chief activity. Traditionally most of their communication has taken place through telephone and telex, and still today these media are mostly used. There seems to be, however, a trend towards the increasing utilization of data transmission through computer networks.

Table XVII US Data Communication Manufacturers, 1979

Computer Front-Ends	Sales in US$ thousands
IBM	157,753
NCR	65,270
Memorex	53,944
Burroughs	24,904
Control Data	24,000
Sperry Univac	23,700
Hewlett Packard	19,765
Honeywell	14,530
Modems/Multiplexors	**Sales in US$ thousands**
Racal-Milgo	96,800
Motorola	73,170
3M	39,120
Rixon Inc.	36,156
General Data Comm.	35,445
Paradyne Corp.	28,980
Racal-Vadic	24,500
Infotron	18,785
Timeplex	13,659

Source: Datamation, ·June 1980.

They share usage of networks that are so expensive that a single company could not afford it.

Membership in the network is therefore of crucial interest for effective and competitive performance.

They also use private networks that may give them considerable competitive advantage vis-à-vis other corporations in the same sector. Large-scale applications of data processing technology are very capital-intensive and likely to be accessible to the largest firms only. Involvement in Electronic Funds Transfer, for example, demands a considerable increase in a bank's up-front investments. Equipment expenses are high and it may well be that after some years the maintenance will be even higher.

The pioneer in transnational data flows has been SITA: the Société International des Télécommunications Aéronautiques. SITA was established in 1949 by 11 airlines as a reservations system using a low-speed teleprinter system. By 1974, 185 airlines from 90 countries were part of the system. The present network is built around nine switching computers in Amsterdam, London, Paris, Frankfurt, Madrid, Rome, New York, Hong Kong and Beirut. Over 200 airlines in some 118 countries participate. SITA comprises over 10,000 teleprinter stations, 2,000 reservation terminals and 20 airline reservation systems.

It is most probable that SITA carries today the largest data volume of any computer network.[14]

Among the heavy data traffic users are also the large international banks, and their case provides a good illustration of the 'lifeblood' category.[15]

Although at present banks in the main use traditional communication media and prefer telex, telephone and mail over the computer network, there are indications that a rapid expansion of the use of computer communication is very likely.[16]

Indications are such that bankers expect that in the next few years the computer will rate highest as communication means and that in West Europe banks already count for the largest share (30%) in network terminating points.[17]

The need for international telecommunication networks has drastically increased with the transnationalisation of banking. During the 1960s and the beginning of the 1970s US banks, followed by the top West European and Japanese banks, spread worldwide.

To adequately respond to the communication needs created by this transnationalisation, the banks created networks for their individual use and for interbank use.

Examples of the first category are the private leased-line telecommunication networks of Chase Manhattan Bank, Bank of America or Citibank. Citibank's

GLOBECOM system stands for a network of leased channels that interconnect the overseas branches of Citibank in some 100 countries. More than 300,000 transmissions per month pass through computer switches in London, Bahrain, Hong Kong and New York. Most of the circuits are low-speed telegraphic circuits. Store and forward switching are the primary means of transmission. Some are SVD circuits, and voice channels on those circuits are used for administrative communication among the different branches. The bulk of the bank's telegraphic and telephone traffic goes through the network. For international loan syndication operations Citibank started in the late 70s an electronic mailing system that uses the Mark III network of General Electric.

The most important example of a network created for interbank use is S.W.I.F.T. (Society for Worldwide Interbank Financial Telecommunications). The idea for S.W.I.F.T. was born in the late 1960s when a group of large West European banks studied the possibility of improved international transaction procedures and came to the conclusion that international banking needed an accurate, rapid, safe and standardized funds transfer system. As a result of the study and the positive response from the banks, the major West European, Canadian and US banks established S.W.I.F.T. in May 1973. Four years later in May 1977 the network became operational. By then almost $1 billion had been spent on the network and equipment was procured from Burroughs, ICL and General Automation. In 1980 S.W.I.F.T. was expected to carry 250,000 messages (each of some 250 characters) daily through its system with which different types of terminals can be connected via leased telecommunication lines or public telephone networks. As S.W.I.F.T. General Manager C. Reuterskiold describes it, "For the first time ever the banking world now has its own fast, reliable, responsive and secure international payment transaction system."[18] An important feature of the system is that it guarantees absolute confidentiality of message transfer with all transmissions over international lines being encrypted. Encryption keys at the ends of each line are changed at random intervals.

S.W.I.F.T. connects through operating centres in Belgium, the Netherlands and the US over 700 banks in 26 countries. Transactions processed fall into four main categories: customer transfers; bank transfers; foreign exchange confirmations; and loan/deposit confirmations.

For interbank communication on the domestic level the largest networks have been created in the US. They are the Federal Reserve System's network, Fed Wire, that serves the Federal Reserve district banks; Bank Wire which is owned by some 200 banks; and the Clearing House Interbank Payments

System (CHIPS) that connects 92 banks in the New York City area. The daily message volume of Fed Wire is 110,000, Bank Wire 20,000 and CHIPS 46,000 (in 1979).

In the daily operations of the banks these systems can all be connected with each other and with S.W.I.F.T.

On several occasions bankers have expressed the opinion that data traffic can indeed be seen as the bank's 'lifeblood'. R. D. Hill, who is Chairman of the First National Bank of Boston, observes, "The degree of information flow among our offices largely determines the degree to which we can actually manage and control our international operations. If we were prevented from moving vital information to headquarters, it could significantly impact our ability to manage the corporation as a total entity."[19]

Data as instrument for management

In this category one finds a variety of transnational corporations that although not as 'data-intensive' as category B are increasingly involved with data transport and data processing. As David Hebditch observes, "This group of companies might just be able to manage without computers. Indeed, in some cases, the level of automation might be relatively low at the present time. However, most of these organisations have sophisticated computer communications networks at a fairly advanced stage of development."[20] As R. V. Austin from Unilever remarks, "The current level of transborder data flow is not high although growing in importance." This is so because Unilever increasingly needs "to communicate information concerning our internal and external business operations between units. For that reason, we are establishing in Europe a private data and voice communications network."[21]

There are as yet no satisfactory figures to give a solid account of how at present corporations in this category are involved with data flows and to project how this will develop.

Satellite Business Systems – the digital communications service by IBM, Aetna and Comsat – certainly expects that the information requirements of large corporations will increasingly have to be met through data networks. SBS promises to enable its customers to:

– Integrate the organisation's diverse communications requirements (for voice, data, facsimile, etc.) into a single, full-switched, centrally managed private network;

- Allocate network capacity dynamically, on a nearly instantaneous basis, to meet shifting demands among network locations;
- Implement new communications applications not previously practical or possible, such as video teleconferencing, high-speed computer-to-computer networking, and high-speed electronic mail; and (as a consequence of these capabilities);
- Exercise better management control over the dispersed activities of the organisation.

From the SBS offering, the expectation can be construed that transnational corporations would through data flows gain considerable savings on their communication services, increase their productivity and improve their flexibility.

It remains to be studied whether these benefits do indeed accrue from the application of computer networks. As was suggested earlier, corporations need information for the "pro-active adaptation to their dynamic environments. This requires management to deal with comparatively uncontrollable, qualitative, external, future-oriented data sources and unaccustomed processes for analysis, simulation and consolidation of diverse data types into management information."[22] This confronts management increasingly with the necessity to access processing systems through which the data are programmed into applicable information. Data as a tool for management requires the installation of decision supporting systems (DSS) and interfaces between DSS and data bases.

Additionally, there is the internal demand for effectively coping with the requirements of a complex organisation. Complexity is introduced due to the volume of operations, the geographical distribution of plants and markets, the diversity of products and services and rapid growth.

There are distinctions in the ways corporations approach the technology related to data flows. There are corporations that apply Management Information Systems based upon advanced data processing technology, merely choosing the most current technology available for the organisational problems they are faced with. The application of technology is only to serve the predetermined corporate strategy.

There are also corporations that are change-oriented and will allow the new technology to have an influence on their corporate strategy. The technology will play an important role in finding new approaches to management problems.

For integrated management – i.e. centralized control and decentralized operations – the new data processing technology offers the necessary flexibility. Large computer systems for central processing can be combined with word processing, electronic mail and videoteleconferencing that enable varying degrees of decentralization.

Data flows in the transnational corporation can generally be seen as performing the following functions:

- support system for management decision-making;
- maintenance services to the firm itself and clients;
- monitoring of inventories and production volumes;
- monitoring of market, price and currency developments;
- transfer of funds – intra- and intercompany;
- intra-company accounting;
- access to scientific/technical data bases;
- transport and processing of R&D data;
- transport and storing of personnel records.

At present, costs involved in computer networks (especially communication tariffs) are still very high and seem to favour the largest corporations in benefitting from transnational data flows.

Projection

It seems likely that corporations presently found in category C will within some years more appropriately be located in category B.

In the information age the majority of transnational corporations will experience data as their 'lifeblood'. This is becoming clearer in the rapidly expanding and internationally spreading services industry. In 1980 the total world trade in services amounted to US$ 400 billion, which is more than 20% of overall world trade. Most of the industries involved with this trade depend heavily on the processing and transmission of data. Examples include technical consultants, software vendors, data processing services, and transportation.

Increasingly, users of transnational data flows are also found in such industrial sectors as automobile manufacturing (particularly for production coordination and inventory monitoring), chemical and pharmaceutical production (particularly for research and development), and in the oil industry (particularly for control over refining, distributing and price-fluctuation monitoring).

There will be still more convergence when overlaps will also show up with category A. Already large data flow users are engaged in the sales of data as an important product-line. Banks, for example, offer huge data banks (e.g. Chase Econometrics) and sell computer services (e.g. Citibank's subsidiary Citishare). In addition, large oil companies own data communication vendors, such as Exxon with its subsidiary Periphonics. And large data communication manufacturers (such as IBM and Motorola) are among the heaviest data network users.

This could point to the formation of a global data market in which production, distribution, transmission, servicing, processing and application of data is effected virtually by a small number of large, vertically integrated transnational corporations.

Notes Chapter 4

1 F. A. Bernasconi in his address to the IBI World Conference on Transborder Data Flow Policies, Rome, June 1980.
2 R. E. L. Walker in his testimony before the Sub-committee on Government Information and Individual Rights of the US House of Representatives Committee on Government Operations, Washington, March 13, 1980.
3 R. W. Langhorne in a paper for *ONLINE, Data regulation,* Uxbridge, 1978, p 141.
4 J. L. Rankine quoted in *Transnational Data Report,* Vol III No 1, 1980.
5 H. I. Schiller, *Who Knows: Information in the Age of the Fortune 500,* Norwood: Ablex Publishing, 1981, pp 36–37.
6 J. K. W. van Leeuwen, 'Ondernemen in Nederland in het Informatietijdperk', in M. Chamalaun (ed), *Het Informatietijdperk,* Amsterdam: *Inter-Mediair,* 1981, pp 14–21.
7 J. M. Treille, *New Strategies for Business Information,* Paris: OECD document DSTI/ICCP/79.19, March 1979, pp 10–12.
8 Ministère de l'Industrie, *Les chiffres clés de l'informatisation,* Paris: La Documentation Française, 1981, p 41.
9 J. M. Treille, o.c., p 12.
10 A. D. Little Inc., *The Netherlands in the Information Age,* The Hague: Centrum voor Informatiebeleid, 1981, p 91.
11 A. R. Berkeley, 'Millionaire Machine?', in *Datamation,* August 25, 1981, pp 20–36.
12 M. Disman, 'Software Trends in Europe', in *Datamation,* August 25, 1981, pp 41–48.
13 According to Laurie, Millbank & Co., in Ministère de l'Industrie, o.c., p 59.

14 Logica Ltd, *The Usage of International Data Networks in Europe,* Paris: OECD, 1979, pp 209–218.

15 For elaborate treatment of banks and information, see C. J. Hamelink, *Finance and Information,* Norwood: Ablex Publishing Corp., 1983.

16 R. H. Veith, *Multinational Computer Nets,* Lexington (Mass.): D. C. Heath & Co., 1981, p 66.

17 M. Benedetti, 'Eurodata '79: the growth of data communications in Western Europe', paper for the IBI World Conference on Transborder Data Flow Policies, Rome, June 1980.

18 In the foreword to the S.W.I.F.T. brochure, 1980, p 3.

19 Source: *Transnational Data Report,* Vol IV No 4, 1981, p 37.

20 D. Hebditch, 'Will data flow be stemmed?' in *Telecommunications,* May 1979, p 75.

21 Source: *Transnational Data Report,* Vol III No 3, 1980.

22 R. Alloway, 'Decision support systems and information flows in the 1980s, in E. J. Boutmy and A. Danthine (eds), *Teleinformatics '79,* Amsterdam: North Holland, 1979, p 4.

5 Impact of Transnational Data Flow

The impact of the utilization of computer networks by transnational corporations can be discussed in terms of the impact on internal environment and external environment.

Internal environment of the corporation

The use of data flows could give the transnational corporation greater capacity to respond to the requirements of its internal environment. It could provide management with a tool to more effeciently and effectively allocate corporate resources: the essence of industrial management. An example would be the allocation of human resources: the international division of labour within the corporation. Data networks facilitate more adequate patterns of job location. As Alain Madec has observed.

> "This often consists in locating industrial jobs in the developing countries, where manpower is cheap, while intellectual jobs are located near to stocks of internal data, or in the place where there is a pressing need for help in decisionmaking, i.e. at headquarters."[1]

The use of data flows could enable transnational corporations to realize economies of scale through the expanding production specialization among their subsidiaries. Data networks could contribute to close coordination between units in geographically widely distributed locations.

The use of data flows could make it possible to cope with the complexity of hierarchically structured management processes which can easily be disturbed by time delays and distortions of less sophisticated communication facilities and by the absence of effective headquarter monitoring facilities. The optimal functioning of the 'centralization-decentralization model' that is characteristic of the transnational corporation, depends upon fast and reliable data networks.

Internationally operating corporations demand both centralization and decentralization in organisation.

– Centralization is necessary to be able to check on the performance of the total corporate system. A financial strategy that demands the assurance of a continuous financing of the trading operations and a protection of the corporate profits needs a continuous and coordinated monitoring of rapidly fluctuating money markets and price developments. Also, centralized information about production is needed to facilitate the international specialization of labour within the corporation.

– Production specialization is a major requirement for transnational corporations and this makes *decentralization* essential for an optimal performance of local/national chapters.

Corporations design *Management Information Systems* to adequately respond to the requirements of the corporate organisation. This is often a laborious task and the centralization-decentralization model creates complicated logistical problems for worldwide corporate information facilities. Potentially transnational data flows could contribute to the solution of such problems. They can function as the management tool that makes this centralization-decentralization model workable. "Management will be able to determine which controls and standards should be applied throughout the organisation to facilitate meaningful corporate control, based on business consideration, rather than the limitations of communication/computing facilities. Planning can be decentralized within meaningful constraints and yet controlled centrally."[2]

At this point it has to be observed that often the expectation is expressed that the wide application of small and cheap computer systems will lead to full decentralization and to the disappearance of large-scale central computer systems. This is very unlikely since even very decentralized corporate organisations will require the capacity to coordinate and consolidate the different types of data that are pertinent to the corporate operation. Also, "the economics of specialized processors and the necessity for a common index of data base locations and contents require the continuation of central installations."[3]

Transnational data flows can theoretically optimise the performance of what Chamoux has referred to as the organisational innovation of the transnational corporation: the 'profit centre'. The local subsidiary is free to fix its policy in order to achieve the goals determined by headquarters. There is decentralized autonomy as long as profits are made. Data traffic is an essential component of this organisational model. There has to be continuous reporting back from subsidiaries to headquarters and a flow of instructions from headquarters to subsidiaries.[4]

Management's effective and efficient decision-making is largely dependent upon information. Decision-making capacity can, however, seriously be hampered if there are no reliable media for storage, distribution and retrieval. Management Information Systems, that have been designed to cope with this, often turned out to have serious shortcomings, such as the fact that they usually do not provide informal data, but mainly quantifiable data, that they are too general and that the data often come too late. Management Information Systems were in the main designed to deal with routine problems, whereas management is constantly confronted with the unusual and unexpected. Potentially, computer-based interactive management information systems could avoid such shortcomings and offer the inclusive, timely, detailed, informal and flexible information tool management needs.

The use of data flows could further contribute to 'computerize' the corporation. In administrative, financial and manufacturing processes data manipulation through computer intelligence could be the core activity and substitute and significantly change human labour. The fact that banks become increasingly involved with computer-communications also has effects on the banks themselves. Electronic funds transfers, computerized tellers and automated administrative procedures may have significant influence on the employment in the banking sector. The Nora/Minc report projects that the installation of new computer systems could lead the banks to need in the next 10 years 30% less personnel.[5]

Summarizing: the growth and productivity of complex organisations such as transnational corporations is a function of their capacity to effectively and efficiently coordinate functionally and geographically diverse operations. This capacity could potentially be enhanced through transnational data flows.

External environment

Impact on the external environment of transnational corporations can be discussed under a number of headings.

Concentration

The basic processes through which industrial concentration takes place: diversification, horizontal and vertical integration can through the use of transnational data flows be facilitated. They all imply complex coordinating tasks and need fast and reliable monitoring of dispersed markets.

At present small and medium-sized companies do not have the same access to data flow facilities as the large transnational data network-users. This tends to give large transnational corporations a vital competitive advantage, and may create serious barriers to new entrants and lead to increasingly oligopolistic markets in different sectors of the economy.

For example: the large-scale application and development of international telecommunication networks is likely to give advantages for large banks against their smaller competitors. According to Rose, the electronic transfer of funds (EFT) will contribute to the raising of savings and will free a considerable amount of human and other resources now locked up in an oversized and inefficient financial industry. He expects, through a redeployment of these sources in sectors of the economy where they can be more profitably used, a rising national output and an increase in the supply of goods and services which will hold down the price level.[6]

The implication of this statement is that EFT will strongly contribute to the concentration of the banking system. EFT will lead to a situation where fewer banks hold the major portion of society's financial assets. An important factor here is the capital intensity of the necessary technological infrastructure and its maintenance. It is likely that the largest banks will be the first to install the most advanced data processing machinery and this could seriously affect the capacity of smaller banks to compete.

The question obviously is whether this will change with decreasing costs for data processing-related equipment and services. So far, it can be observed that cost reductions have mainly been to the benefit of the largest users. It can be expected that the costs of long-line services for data flows within the corporation will decrease for the large transnational users. At the same time it seems that costs of local data transport do not decrease at a similar pace, thus making access to data networks for the small users very difficult. Cost reductions are also not likely to affect large-scale equipment and related programming and maintenance expenses, thus leaving them mainly to the largest corporations.

Standardization

The need for centralized data processing may lead to the wish to install standardized equipment in the dispersed units. This could tend to further strengthen the oligopolistically structured computer and telecommunication industry.

Regulatory environment

The large transnational data flow users have important stakes in the free flow of data across borders and are likely to attempt to influence their environment for the appropriate deregulation. As IBM President John Opel states, "Except when it threatens privacy and national security, data flow should be as uninhibited as possible."[7]

John Diebold, Chairman of the Diebold Group Inc., explains the consequences if a free flow of data is not secured: "Dramatic reductions in the rapidly growing information sectors of the United States economy and increased costs and poorer service to all international users; higher costs for long haul and overseas communications; serious reduction of information available in the United States about the rest of the world."[8]

Private circuits

Telecommunication is a vital part of transnational data flows and a worrying item for transnational corporations. Telecommunication tariffs are an important factor in the use of computer networks, and prices determined by national political and economic considerations can restrict data flows.[9]

As a consequence, transnational corporations will emphasize the need of privately leased circuits with volume-insensitive tariff systems. As Phillip Onstad, Control Data Corporation's Manager of Telecommunication Policies, claims, if such circuits are not available "advances in distributed processing and shared data base developments will be severely retarded. In addition, the effectiveness of many existing teleprocessing systems will be degraded, and in many instances their services will have to be withdrawn."[10] This particular need of the largest data flow users could have a serious impact on the revenues of national public telecommunication services.

Division of labour

Transnational data flows are likely to encourage transnational corporations to apply the theory of 'comparative advantage' also to the field of advanced information technology. In terms of this theory each nation contributes to the international exchange what it can produce most advantageously.

The availability of satellite communication plus inexpensive terminals for remote accessing of large data bases and large computer systems tends to lead to the concentration of data processing in relatively few locations. Data processing is done where it can be most cost-effectively carried out: in US-owned facilities.

The Canadian case provides an example. Through the transfer of data processing to the US, by 1975 4,000 jobs were lost. By 1980 this had increased to 10,000 and was expected to reach 25,000 in 1985.[11]

Transnational data flows could provide corporate management with a tool to more efficiently and effectively allocate the human resources within the corporation. Using this tool transnational corporations will be inclined to maintain their core activities, administratively, financially and technologically, close to headquarter locations, and keep that part of the industrial production in developing countries that does not improve the trading prospects of these countries.

A likely construction is the location of R&D intensive parts of industrial production in the developed world and the manufacturing of end-products in the developing countries. "The decreasing cost of communications and data transmission and the concentration of information in developed countries implies that it is becoming cheaper for enterprises and firms in developing countries to 'solve' problems in a remote location rather than through the development of local facilities."[12]

Informatisation of society

There is a lot of speculation as to the structure of the 'information society' by the year 2000.

Among all the different futurologies most solid looks the expectation that the informatisation of society will make it considerably more vulnerable. The Nora/Minc report also points to this as a key feature of future developments. The vulnerability will be created, i.a. because information traffic tends to become so intensive, voluminous and complex that decisions about it have to be delegated to electronic systems that are often located in foreign countries and that have such complex constructions that even the experts can hardly check what the system has calculated. This leads all information-related activities to become dependent upon automated, often highly centralized systems that may easily be deranged.

The complexity of the electronic systems may lead to a dependence upon systems that can only be effectively controlled by themselves. Moreover, computers can transform increasing loads of data into increasing loads of information. Thus, scarcity of information transforms into overload of information, creating a different type of scarcity: time to process the information overload. This in turn necessitates more information to be processed by the electronic system. This could increase the need for pre-programmed information and standardized problem solutions. More parts of decision-making procedures would then be delegated to the electronic intelligence. Information-overload is also created by the increased rapidity of the information traffic. With increasing rates at which information is delivered, the time for adequate transformation in decision-making decreases. If it is true as Bernasconi expects that the increasing use of data flows is a stimulus towards the development of an informatised society, the role of the largest users is paramount.[13] They will handle most of the data upon which national economies become dependent, they own and operate the data bases where sensitive data will be stored, they operate the networks through which much of the data transport is done, they control the data processing facilities upon which others will be dependent.

National sovereignty

National sovereignty can be defined as the capacity to influence allocative decisions regarding national resources. Transnational data flows tend to export data relevant to such allocative decisions beyond the jurisdiction of national governments.

Transnational data flows imply thus the risk that crucial decision-making is governed by actors in other countries.

Concentration of data processing facilities in only a few countries with transnational corporations and the concurrent loss of economic opportunities, the lagging behind of R&D capacity and the lack of control over data imports, exports and application tend to create a serious diminishing of sovereignty in processes of decision-making. Control over the locations where data processing and data storage are executed is an important factor affecting the control over decisions. If a country lacks data about itself – whether because it has no capacity to collect them or because it has no capacity to process them – it lacks pertinent decision-making capacity about its own existence.

"This can result in a national self-perception of impotence, an inability to effect one's vital choices, and the effective erosion of one's political sovereignty."[14] If a foreign entity possesses the data and the resulting information/knowledge (such as in the case of mineral-exploiting corporations versus mineral-holding developing countries), decision-making capacity is extra-territorially located and national sovereignty subverted.

If it can be assumed that transnational corporations play a significant role in the economies of their host countries, it follows that they collect volumes of data pertinent to these countries. These data will be processed and held abroad. This leaves national governments at a disadvantage both vis-à-vis the domestic economy and the transnational corporation. To exercise jurisdiction over a company that operates on the national territory but processes and stores its vital data elsewhere becomes a serious problem.

Transnational data flows, for example, imply increasing chances to escape governmental control on the international flow of capital. It has always been very difficult for governments to control capital flows, but the advanced information technology challenges the national sovereign powers most fundamentally. A good example provides the Euromarket: the pool of stateless cash that finds its origin in the 1950s and 1960s when the governments of the UK and the US tried to restrict the role of their national currencies in international trade transactions and placed ceilings on rates of interests in support of their domestic economies. The money supply simply shifted from national markets to a newly created uncontrolled Euromarket. The estimated $1 trillion pool has created a new source of investment capital and has certainly contributed to more international trade. For commercial bankers the Euro-currency market supplies crucial investment funds for transnational corporations and provides the mechanism through which OPEC countries can trade their petrodollars. For most governments the Euromarket is, as Italy's former central banker G. Carli describes it, "The root of evil in the international monetary system."[15] It is seen to contribute largely to financial instability and to disrupt national attempts to curb inflation. Information technology plays an important role. The possibility to trade currencies practically instantaneously creates monetary instability and can easily drive down a currency's value.

Most of the Euromarket transactions occur electronically and this is a major reason for the diminishing potential of governments to control them. As Citibank's Vice President W. Sparks concludes, "The Euromarket is a paradigm of what happens when governments attempt to control the flow of capital in the new era of international communication."[16] The application of modern information technology tends to increase the power of the trans-national banks vis-à-vis the power of national governments.

Transnational data flows can be protected from any control. Technically this is possible, since random routing through different parts of the network, direct transmission via satellites or encryption make any form of border control on transnational data flows futile.

Cultural synchronization

If transnational data flows are seen as an additional component in the international communication structure, it follows that this advanced techno-logical facility could further strengthen the present pattern of cultural impact. As has been documented elsewhere, the international flow of communication is largely controlled by a small number of Western transnational industrial conglomerates. The majority of the world's communication equipment (satellites, radio and tv sets, telex, etc.), patents on communication technol-ogy, and communication products (films, tv programmes, comics, etc.) originates in what can be called the information industrial complex. This complex steers the global flow of communication because of its access to finance, technology and marketing: the three pillars of power in the present world order.[17]

This communication control represents the cultural component of the pattern of international disparities. The international flow of communication has in fact become the main carrier of global cultural synchronization. The process of cultural synchronization draws information-dependent countries into a homogeneity created by the life styles, consumption modes and symbolic values of the information-independent countries.   •

It seems logical to expect that transnational data flows would contribute to this process since they are, due to technological convergences, structurally similar to other communication channels.

Global use of data flows – particularly through transnational corporations – is thus likely to have an impact on the synchronization of techniques (e.g. via the standardization of equipment), symbols (e.g. through the use of the universal computer language) and social relations (e.g. through the organis-ation of industrial production and job patterns).

Information disparity

The large-scale application of data processing technology by transnational corporations will further increase their informational advantage over the nations of the developing world. This would concur with the observation that the application of computer capacity tends to lead to a new social disparity: between the information-rich and the information-poor. A disparity not in the sense of access to physical volumes of information, but in the sense of processing capacity.

As was pointed out before, the lack of access to essential components of the capacity to manipulate data gives developing countries a serious disadvantage in their negotiating positions vis-à-vis foreign industrial and financial corporations. A particular problem poses the category of scientific/technical information. The use of computer networks can enhance the R&D capacity of transnational corporations and makes technological competition illusory for small and medium-sized companies in developing countries.

Notes Chapter 5

1 A. J. Madec, *Economic and Legal Aspects of Transborder Data Flow,* paper for the High Level Conference on Information, Computer and Communication Policies in the 1980s, OECD, Paris, October 1980.

2 D. A. Woodland and P. S. Doepel, 'Management of Distributed Organisations', in E. J. Boutmy and A. Danthine (eds), *Teleinformatics '79,* Amsterdam: North Holland, 1979, p 10.

3 R. Alloway, 'Decision Support Systems and Information Flow in the 80s', in E. J. Boutmy and A. Danthine, o.c., p 5.

4 J. P. Chamoux, *L'information sans frontière,* Paris: La Documentation Française, 1980, p 90.

5 S. Nora and A. Minc, *L'informatisation de la société,* Paris: La Documentation Française, 1978, p 36.

6 S. Rose, 'The unexpected fallout from electronic banking', in *Fortune,* April 24, 1978.

7 Source: *Transnational Data Report,* Vol II No 5, 1979.

8 Source: *Transnational Data Report,* Vol III No 1, 1980.

9 'Going Global' in *Datamation,* September 1980; D. Hebditch, 'Will data flow be stemmed?', in *Telecommunications,* May 1979, p 75.

10 Source: *Transnational Data Report,* Vol II No 5, 1979.

11 P. Robinson, 'The Economic Impact of TDF', paper for the IBI World Conference on Transborder Data Flow Policies, Rome, June 1980.

12 J. F. Rada, *Micro-electronics, Information Technology and its Effects on Developing Countries,* Geneva: ILO, 1980, p 29.

13 F. A. Bernasconi, *IBI Newsletter,* No 34, 1980, p 34.

14 A. Gotlieb, Ch. Dalfen and K. Katz, 'The Transborder Transfer of Information by Communications and Computer Systems', in *The American Journal of International Law,* Vol 68 No 2, April 1974, p 247.

15 G. Carli, quoted in *TIME,* November 5, 1979, p 60.

16 W. Sparks, 'The Flow of Information and the New Technology of Money', address at the Conference on World Communications: Decisions for the Eighties, Philadelphia, May 1980.

17 For more documentation and analysis of international communication control and cultural synchronization, see C. J. Hamelink, *The Corporate Village,* Rome: IDOC, 1977, and C. J. Hamelink, *Cultural Autonomy in Global Communications,* New York: Longman, 1983.

6 Disparities in Telematics Infrastructure

Today the main beneficiaries of transnational data flows are located in North America, West Europe and Japan. For the rest of the world, and particularly for developing countries, participation in telematics is problematic since the infrastructural conditions are very unevenly divided.

Availability of computers

Disparities can clearly be illustrated from the availability of computers in the world. In 1975 developing countries had less than 3% of the world's general-purpose computers installed. The US and West Europe had some 57%. According to a survey at the end of 1976 the installation of computers was in terms of monetary value distributed as follows: the US accounted for 45.5%, industrialized countries together 87.1%, socialist countries 6.7% and developing countries approximately 5%.[1]

In 1979 the total monetary value of installed computers reached US$ 25 billion. The US represented $11.1 billion, West Europe $7.7 billion, and Japan $4.1 billion. This amounts to almost 92%.[2]

An indication of disparity is also provided by the distribution of informatics expenditures. This is the total of national expenses for data processing-linked equipment, personnel, services and transmission channels. In 1979 the US, Japan, West Germany, France and the UK accounted for over 80% of the world's informatics expenditure. The socialist countries accounted for almost 4% and the rest of the world shared some 12%.[3]

Telecommunication investments

In the field of telecommunication, disparities between the North and the South are already given with the distribution of telephones. In 1979 the total number of telephones in service in the US and West Europe was 329.3 million, the total for Africa and Latin America 21.7 million.[4]

A measure of disparity is also given with the differential utilization of available telecommunication facilities, such as satellite services. At the beginning of 1980 almost half the telecommunication capacity of the International Tele-communications Satellite Organisation (INTELSAT) was used by only five countries (US, UK, West Germany, France and Japan).[5]

Disparity shows also in the distribution of investments for telecommunication. In 1968 developed countries could invest $16.60 per capita of the population and this increased to $54.40 in 1977. Developing countries invested in 1968 $1.60 per capita of the population and in 1977 $6.70. Taking telecommuni-cation investments per annum as a percentage of GDP gives another index of disparity. In developed countries in the period 1965–1975 investments were on average 0.90% of GDP; in developing countries this was 0.35%.[6]

In 1976 the US accounted for almost 52% of the world's telecommunication investments and seven West-European countries (UK, West Germany, France, Italy, Sweden, the Netherlands, Belgium) accounted for over 18%. The rest of West Europe, the socialist countries and developing countries shared some 14%. Projections for 1985 expect a share for the US and the seven West-European countries reaching over 75%.[7]

Information technology trade

Disparities are strongly present in the international trade in information technology products and services.

In 1980 the world market for telecommunication equipment reached an estimated US$ 40 billion. The combined share for Africa and Latin America was US$1.4 billion.[8]

In terms of the international trade in computer products and services the US and West Europe are by far the largest exporters and importers. Figures for 1978 for computer and office equipment world import markets show a share for West Europe and the US of 71% and for developing countries of 10.2%.[9]

In 1979 US computer exports were 54% to West Europe and 12% to Canada. French exports were 85% to other West-European countries and 5% to the US. British exports were 79% to other West-European countries and 8% to the US. US imports were 23% from the UK, France and West Germany. West German imports were 71% from the US, UK and France. French imports were 73% from the US, UK and West Germany.[10]

Most international computer trade takes place within and between West Europe and North America. These trading patterns are corroborated by an increasing number of know-how exchange agreements that have been signed over the past years. Examples include arrangements between the General Electric Corporation in the UK and Fairchild in the US, between Siemens (West Germany) and Advanced Micro Devices (US), between Thomson CSF (France) and Motorola (US), and between Philips (the Netherlands) and Signetics (US).

It has to be observed, however, that the developing world is gaining importance as a computer import market.[11] Between 1972 and 1975 average annual imports grew in Asia by 13.9% (with evidently the leading role for an industrialized nation, Japan), Africa by 44.2% and Latin America by 38%. During the 1970s Latin America became the largest importer in the South, especially with countries such as Chile and Cuba reaching import growth percentages of respectively 202% and 97%.

Also in the second half of the 1970s Latin-American imports continued to grow, although slightly less, but still above the world average rate of growth (this was for the 1977–1978 period, 28.2%). Brazil is becoming the leading computer importer of the region and in 1978 this country was the 16th largest computer market in the world with a growth rate of 43.3%. Mexico is the 20th largest importer, Argentina and Venezuela are respectively numbers 24 and 26.

Among the fastest growing import markets is now also the People's Republic of China. Its 1977–1978 growth rate was 164% and its market size passed the 21 million-dollar mark.

Also, over the past years, the developing countries' share in imports by OECD countries of office machines, telecommunication equipment and semiconductors has rapidly grown.[12] For telecommunication equipment the share of OECD imports from developing countries increased from 3.5% in 1965 to 18.7% in 1977. For electronic components the share of OECD imports from developing countries increased from 2.2% in 1965 to 29% in 1977. It should be noted, however, that the imports came predominantly from a limited number of countries with very narrow ranges of specialization in specific products. Moreover, this production was mainly a result of foreign investments. Eight countries accounted for more than 90% of the increase of OECD imports of electronic goods from developing countries between 1970 and 1976. These were Mexico, Brazil, Malaysia, India, Singapore, Korea, Taiwan and Hong Kong.

This reflects the general pattern of direct foreign investment that tends to be limited (for approximately 70%) to a selected number of (some 15) countries that are chosen for their political stability, economic incentives (such as tax privileges, large domestic markets, and low wages), and linguistic convenience (anglophone countries have clear preference). In the period 1970–1976 six countries (South Korea, Taiwan, Hong Kong, Singapore, Mexico and Brazil) represented almost 70% of the total of developing countries' exports of manufactured goods.

The countries from which the majority of OECD imports of electronic goods came specialized in specific products, such as Taiwan in television receivers, Korea in electronic components, and Mexico in switch gears. This reflects the strategy of transnational corporations to select those products for foreign investment that need unskilled labour in a specific (isolated) phase of the production process, that demand little investment in fixed assets and imply low costs for transportation of the intermediate goods between headquarters and offshore plants. Particularly in the manufacturing of electronic equipment, developing countries get only one stage in a vertically integrated and centrally controlled operation.

Most of the imports reflected particular geographic patterns. Mexico, Taiwan and Hong Kong accounted for over 50% of US imports. Hong Kong, Taiwan and Singapore accounted for almost 70% of the EEC imports and Korea, Taiwan and Singapore for some 80% of Japanese imports. These patterns represent flows of foreign direct investments. Almost 80% of US imports from the eight countries are in fact related to intra-firm transactions.[13] Exports from these low-wage countries in the majority result from the investments large transnational electronics manufacturers make in offshore production and assembly operations by their subsidiaries.

This again reflects the general pattern of international trade in which some 30% is related to intra-firm transactions by transnational corporations.

Notes Chapter 6

1 International Commission for the Study of Communication Problems, *Many Voices, One World,* Paris: UNESCO, 1980, p 130.
2 Ministère de l'Industrie, *Les chiffres-clés de l'informatisation,* Paris: La Documentation Française, 1980, p 54.
3 Ibidem, p 15.
4) Source: AT&T, quoted in *The Economist,* August 22, 1981.

5 Source: *Media-Info,* published by VNU, Amsterdam, Vol I No 20, July 17, 1981.

6 International Commission for the Study of Communication Problems, o.c., p 131.

7 Ministère de l'Industrie, o.c., p 61.

8 Source: Arthur D. Little, quoted in *The Economist,* August 22, 1981.

9 Sources: *Datamation,* March 1978, July 1980, January 1981; Ministère de l'Industrie, o.c.; C. J. Hamelink, *Finance and Information,* Norwood: Ablex Publishing, 1983.

10 Ibidem.

11 *Datamation,* January, 1981.

12 OECD, *The role of information goods and services in international trade,* paper prepared for the OECD working party on Information, Computer and Communications Policy, Paris, May 1979, pp 36–41.

13 P. A. Blesch, *Developing Countries' Exports of Electronics and Electrical Engineering Products,* Washington: World Bank, 1978.

7 Transnational Data Flows and the Third World

"Africa should choose telematics for its future."
Bukasa Bukasa, Zaire

Confronted with the problems implied in information disparity, developing countries are presently looking for solutions. In this search a strong drive to create telematics capacity has emerged in many developing countries. Most of them, however, have no ability to generate the technology themselves and are dependent upon the North-South transfer of telematics-related technology. This transfer is characterized by the following dimensions:

1 the strong oligopoly in the production of this technology which makes the acquiring parties dependent upon very few suppliers;
2 the transfer of obsolete technology which in itself may not always be disadvantageous, given national objectives, but which demands a rather sophisticated assessment procedure;
3 the lack of specialized expertise for the integration of the technology and the generation of innovations which is even stronger than in other information technologies;
4 the common practice of delivery of relatively cheap systems which offers decreasing hardware prices together with large and profitable software contracts.

It may not be advisable for developing countries to completely ignore new developments in information technology, but given earlier experiences their introduction would minimally ask for a careful and critical weighing of costs and benefits.

Information technology and social development

It is a rather common claim that the introduction of new information technologies – like television, viewdata, microcomputers – will fundamentally change existing social structures.[1] Such technological determinism has also prevailed in much of the development debate. Particularly the adherents to the so-called 'modernization paradigm' believe(d) that the introduction of modern information technology could drastically enhance the process of development through its contribution to the creation of new social structures that would adequately respond to the needs of the developing countries.

The determinists have, however, chosen the wrong order. Information technology is designed and applied to meet those needs that are defined as important by the existing social structure. Just as technology at large is a response to the hierarchy of social needs as it is determined by the existing social order. It is this order that will integrate and guide the development of the technology. Therefore, information technology will rather reinforce existing social structures than transform them.[2]

Raymond Williams, commenting on the development of television technology, writes, "The decisive and earlier transformation of industrial production, and its new social forms, which had grown out of a long history of capital accumulation and working technical improvements, created new needs but also new possibilities, and the communications systems, down to television, were their intrinsic outcome."[3]

In most developing countries the general pattern has been that information technology was not primarily introduced to meet the basic needs of their populations, but as the support system for expanding transnational business.

Looking closely at the distribution of social benefits as resulting from utilization of new information technology, it has to be observed that they normally do not befall the poor majority of the Third World. Studies on the deployment of technologies, such as telephony, educational television and satellite communications in developing countries have suggested that the primary beneficiaries are foreign and national elites, that intended development objectives were not achieved, that unforeseen secondary effects occurred for which no adequate institutional context was present, and that the capital intensity of the new technologies would lead to serious balance-of-payment problems.[4] The case of Algeria is illustrative. In the 1960s the Algerian Government hoped to speed up the country's development process through more effective and expanded telecommunication networks. However, the stated objectives of decentralization of government administration and of more equal income distribution were not achieved. Rather, the national telecommunication infrastructure became increasingly controlled by the foreign suppliers, such as ITT, GT&E, Ericsson and Nippon Electric. Moreover, the acquiring of hardware and related maintenance services caused heavy demands on foreign exchange and called for foreign financiers. Thirdly, the domestic social class benefitting most from the actual use of the new technology was a new bureaucratic elite related to the central government administration.

In short: the advent of new information technology mainly corroborated existing relations of power in society. Therefore, the far-reaching promises which often accompany the introduction of information technology in developing countries have to be looked at very critically. An illustration provides the case of satellite communication. The experiment with instructional television satellite in India (SITE), which was launched in 1975, had among its objectives, the improvement of family planning, agricultural practices, health and hygiene, and a contribution towards national integration, education and teacher training. The Indian communication researcher K. E. Eapen, analyzing the experiment, comments, "The assumption that a professionally competent team of communicators could effectively put across messages, if only necessary technology were at their disposal, did not prove true on the touchstone of SITE. The many persuasive arguments in support of complex delivery systems for effective communication purposes in essentially illiterate societies did not stand up to this experiment . . . SITE exploded the myth that facilities, if made available, will be used, or that they will be used in the way that is intended. When new media are introduced, they appear to fit into existing communication and behavioural patterns rather than radically altering them."[5]

Satellite communication has been proposed to the developing countries with the promising perspective of improved communications for both point-to-point messages and mass distribution in countries with a paucity of terrestrial communications and where the installation of networks of underground cables and microwave relay stations would create insurmountable financial burdens. The implied suggestion was that expanded and effective telecommunication infrastructures would lessen foreign dependence and foster national integration. Yet, as the Algerian case seems to indicate, the new telecommunication network might as well contribute to national disintegration by further widening gaps between the rural poor and the active users of the networks, the urban elites.

In a way, one could even argue that the advent of more advanced telecommunication facilities, such as satellites, have reversed a trend towards increasing national control by developing countries over their telephony and telegraph networks that used to be monopolized by US, French and British cable and wireless corporations. Moreover, the use of satellite communication facilities does not necessarily include its national control. Indonesia, for example, now has its own satellite system with the Palapa I and II, manufactured by Hughes Aircraft. It leases also communications capacity to other nations. Yet, as a representative of Hughes Aircraft admitted, the

Palapa system can be switched off when so requested by Hughes or by the US Defence Department.[6]

In this respect a proposal by the Carter Administration, only withdrawn under heavy pressure, is interesting. The proposal implied the interruption of Iran's use of the INTELSAT communication satellites. Meant as a sanction against Iran, this would disrupt telephone and television services, airline and banking operations. The US National Security Council claimed that such an interruption would find support in the United Nations Charter where communication breaks are seen as legitimate tools for sanctions.

An often suggested benefit to developing nations is the access to vast information resources through remote sensing: the collection from outer space of data by photo satellites about the nation's natural resources. These sensing satellites make data available, through which construction sites that are vulnerable to seismic disturbances can early be detected, suitable land for crop cultivation can be indicated, or the movements of fish in territorial waters can be followed. All apparently attractive assets for a developing country. Yet, on balance, remote sensing may turn out to be more of a liability.

Although the primary data collected by the satellites are now made available to all 'sensed' countries at low prices, the remote sensing bestows the greatest advantages upon those who have the adequate infrastructures for early access to data, their critical selection, their processing into analyzed information and their application. Such infrastructures are accessible to the large transnational explorers and exploiters of energy and mineral resources and not to the developing countries. Oil companies, for example, have early access to data on resource locations and similarly to the expertise needed to assess the pertinence of gathered data. They also have the equipment and analytical skill needed for the processing of data into usable information. And even if the analyzed information were available to all parties concerned, the potential for operating with that information differs greatly. The comparison of relative power between, for example, mineral-holding Zambia and mineral-exploiting Anaconda Copper in terms of access to transnational networks for finance, transportation, and marketing should make this sufficiently clear.

In summary, it can then be said that contrary to many expectations the combination of information technology and development does not necessarily capacitate the South to meet its most fundamental problems and may rather add to the obstacles for its development.

Telematics

Those who argue in favour of developing countries' participation in telematics will usually offer the following benefits:

a. Telematics will enhance participation in the international travel business as well as in international financial transactions.
b. Computer services can boost the productivity of domestic industries and improve their competitive position.
c. The duplication of data banks and data bases would be a waste of resources.
d. Telematics gives access to essential data held abroad.
e. It saves resources if data processing can be done abroad more cheaply than at home.
f. One can use the expertise available in foreign data processing facilities.
g. Through the data collected by resource-sensing satellites, sites vulnerable to seismic disturbances can be detected and suitable land for crop cultivation can be indicated.
h. Educational facilities can be improved through access to more ample teaching materials (tele-education).
i. Health-care facilities can be improved by accessing the best possible resources (tele-medicine).
j. Government administration can be improved through the remote accessing of the best available information resources.

Most of these declared benefits tend to see telematics as an efficient instrument for the integration of the South in the existing world economic order. They seem to be based on a North-South cooperation model that is guided by the concept 'interdependence'. Also they seem to conceive the extraterritorially located information resources as rather neutral developmental tools. Apart from the question which development objectives are served by this position, the benefits it proposes should be balanced against the likely costs.

a. Telematics seems to favour the concentration of data processing-related technology in a few developed countries. This tends to increase the existing technological gap between developed and developing countries.
b. Data processing skills are usually not available in developing countries, and the dependence upon foreign expertise may also imply that such skills will not be developed. This reduces the R&D capacity of developing countries.
c. Since transnational corporations are the largest users of telematics, it follows that their production and marketing strategies will determine the direction of data flows. Raw data (the resources) will tend to flow from

the South to the North and processed data (information packages) will flow from the North to the South.

d. The exporting of raw data and importing of processed data leaves developing countries with a share in the international data trade that will accentuate their balance-of-payment problems. Through the unequal price level between the almost free data and the priced information, their external debt will tend to be aggravated.

e. Developing countries will not be able to exert influence on the price setting. Therefore, prices could be higher if transnational corporations face no serious domestic competition, and could be lower if this serves the purposes of obstructing domestic efforts at establishing data processing capacity. If the processed data are returned at lower prices than the local data processing facility would have to ask, this obstructs domestic data processing facilities.

f. The resources that can be mobilized for the use of remote-sensing data are very unevenly divided between the developing countries and transnational corporations. The equipment and analytical skill involved in the processing of the data is mainly US-owned and rests with large industrial corporations. They include the manufacturers of the hardware for data processing and the ('value-added') information corporations that provide the service of processing the data into information.

g. Even on the simplest technical level there is a serious question as to how developing countries could cope with telematics, given the fact of their generally poorly developed telecommunication infrastructures and the paucity of their electricity supply.

Given the present situation the participation of developing countries in telematics would force them to pay a large price: dependence on foreign equipment suppliers and information producers, loss of vital national information, underdevelopment of R&D capacity. This amounts to the loss of the capability to manage national affairs in a sovereign way: development becomes dependent upon allocative decisions taken outside the national territory.

Could then developing countries avoid these deleterious effects and still have some of the potential benefits? Here the analogy with the European situation could be useful. The European Commission has pleaded that it should be a priority for West Europe to have a minimal dependence upon foreign data processing sources. Therefore, the development of a European information industry has been strongly promoted.[7] This is based on the consideration that the viability of information societies lies primarily in the existence of national industries which can cater to local needs and which can develop expert capacity.

The question is whether this can be applied to developing countries. Some countries, like for example Brazil, are indeed trying to go this road. They are building indigenous infrastructures that give them the basis to "join the interdependent club."[8]

Although this may indeed bring short-term benefits, one would have to question what the long-term impact will be. Could not joining the 'interdependents' obscure existing disparities and even create new ones: between the newly interdependent countries and the not yet interdependent countries?

Does not interdependence imply the integration in a system of international relations that functions against the very interests of developing countries?

The transnational computer networks, for example, are designed to meet the needs of developed countries, and should developing countries not design networks that meet their own needs?

Information technology cannot be isolated from the overall pattern of economic relationships within which it is produced and applied.

And the adopting and even adapting of the technology will by itself not necessarily change the pattern of these relationships.

If a country would want to function within this pattern a possible route might indeed be to join the 'interdependent club' through strong efforts at development of a national telematics capacity that permits participation in transnational data networks. A deceptive notion that tends to be associated with the creation of such capacity is the possibility that this might narrow the North-South technology gap.

It is an illusion to think that developing countries could catch up or keep pace with the advances in telematics technology the North generates. The rate of development of this technology is very high and is supported by resources that developing countries are unable to match. It is a waste of their scarce resources to attempt to follow a 'catching-up strategy' which eventually only benefits the Northern designers and operators of the technology. As H.I. Schiller writes, "Entering the race serves a purpose. It fixes the participant into an enduring relationship of dependence."[9]

It is more realistic to expect that the North-South technology gap will even widen during the decades ahead. As the President of the British Computing Society comments, "It seems likely that the technology gap can never be bridged. The cost of setting out on a technological development path and catching up with the world leaders would be outside the capability of practically any nation." And he concludes, "There must in the future always be some major dependence upon the most advanced nations."[10]

Whether the existence and widening of the technology gap really matters will ultimately depend upon the model of social development a nation chooses.

If developing countries consider the current pattern of international relations detrimental to their self-reliant development, then they will have to fundamentally confront the possibility of another development strategy: one that would concentrate on the satisfaction of a society's basic needs. The point of departure would then be that data and information are important to society's functioning, but that their importance has to be related to the specific needs and priorities of that society. This would have implications for the kinds of data a country would want to collect, their volume, their mode of processing and possibly their mode of transmission (e.g. not under all circumstances would the faster channels be the most wanted).

If from the perspective of 'another development strategy' developing countries would consider the design and application of telematics under their sovereign control, there would still remain complicated problems to face.

Informatics and telecommunication capacity

– A basic condition for telematics is the presence of a reliable and universal electricity supply, a reliable and universal telephone service, and a reliable and universal maintenance service. Already the paucity of electricity supply in many developing countries poses serious handicaps for effective telematics. Developing countries have still less than 10% of the world's telephones and in most rural areas there is less than one telephone per 1,000 inhabitants. There is an overall lack of trained personnel for the maintenance of telephone services.

– Telecommunication facilities are being expanded and upgraded in many developing countries. This usually does not include the installation of the high-capacity telecommunication services telematics demands. Moreover, it hardly occurs as a South-South venture and tends to continue dependence upon Northern suppliers and financiers.[11]

– For terrestrial telecommunications the installation of the technique most suited for data traffic, 'fibre optics', will in most developing countries not become feasible for decades.

– Presently, domestic satellite projects in developing countries are in different stages of development and application, and a number of regional satellite communication projects have been planned.[12] The most vital decisions affecting the developing countries' access to frequencies and services which were expected to be taken at the 1979 World Administrative Radio Conference have been postponed and await further conferences.[13]

– The fact that WARC '79 decided to hold a series of satellite planning conferences is an important break-up of the conventional ITU principle 'first come, first served.' Yet, whether pertinent improvements can be achieved will depend upon the technical expertise the developing countries can mobilize and coordinate in the preparation of these planning conferences.

– For regional satellite systems a potential obstacle is the fact that most participants are members of INTELSAT. In order to keep the system functioning in a profitable way the INTELSAT agreement has built in a limitation for member states wanting to exploit independent systems. Article XIV (on rights and obligations of members) states that for the requiring or utilizing of space-segment facilities separate from INTELSAT, consultation is necessary with the Board of Governers and the Assembly of Parties: "to ensure technical compatibility of such facilities and their operation with the use of the radio frequency spectrum and orbital space by the existing or planned INTELSAT space segment and to avoid significant economic harm to the global system of INTELSAT."

– International support for telecommunication facilities in developing countries is not very generous (see Table XVIII). In 1979 UNDP funds for telecommunications (channelled through the ITU) amounted to US$ 20.7 million. This was however a good 30% more than in 1978.

The limited allocation of funds for telecommunications reflects a hesitation based upon the observation that expansion of telecommunication networks tends to further benefit the already well-off in developing countries. It also reflects national priority setting. In many developing countries the national planning agencies do not rank telecommunications among the first needs.

Table XVIII Lending for Telecommunication by World Bank and IDA: 1976–1980

(in US$ millions)

Borrowers	1976	1977	1978	1979	1980
East Africa	–	–	–	20.0	–
West Africa	5.2	–	–	–	–
East Asia Pacific	31.0	–	–	90.0	–
South Asia	–	80.0	134.5	–	65.0
Europe/M. East/N. Africa	28.0	–	53.0	–	22.0
L. America/Caribbean	–	60.0	33.6	–	44.0
Telecommunication	64.2	140.0	221.1	110.0	131.0
Total Lending	6,632.4	7,066.8	8,410.7	10,010.5	11,481.7
Telecommunication lending in %	1%	2%	3%	1%	1%

Source: Constructed from WORLD BANK Annual Report 1980.

Network problems

– In a number of developing countries public data networks are being planned or are already operational.[14] Their main drawback, as in developed countries, is that they are not really public, like telephony is, at least in developed countries. There are no public terminals and public directories with numbers and call procedures.

Data networks face considerable problems and frustrations in developed countries. This is only worse in developing countries. Among the 'plagues of the 80s' (L. Pouzin) are: antiquated switching plants, incorrect or busy numbers, disconnections, high long distance telephone charges, maximum speeds inadequate for display terminals. Present data circuits are still very unreliable. Between France and the US circuits break down at least once an hour. This instability is expected to last for another 10 years.

Characteristic also of the advanced international data networks is what Pouzin has called "the built-in irresponsibility of international communications": the almost total lack of support for the users. If something goes wrong the carriers will blame this on their competitors.[15]

Data banks

– Data banks pose serious problems if they are created extraterritorially. Since information content is inseparable from its mode of organization, Nora and Minc have rightly stated that the installing of data banks is an imperative of national sovereignty.[16] However, installing national data banks is expensive; it needs sophisticated users and demands advanced organisational contexts.[17]

Informatics and social progress

– In many developing countries informatics is already widely applied in public administration, economic development and production control.

According to an IBI survey, out of a sample of 43 developing countries 34 have 'imperative' or 'incitement' policies for the utilization of informatics in public administration.[18]

At the 1978 Intergovernmental Conference on Strategies and Policies for Informatics (SPIN I) the majority of participants claimed, "Informatics is an instrument ideally suited to the promotion of economic and social development." Informatics was seen, also by representatives from developing countries, as "an undisputed factor of progress."[19] If one, however, critically analyzes the kind of 'progress' the rapidly increasing utilization of informatics supports in the developed countries, it is an act of sheer irresponsibility to suggest a similar path to the developing countries.

– In developed countries it can be observed that the widespread utilization of informatics:

- offers some new job opportunities but on balance creates more unemployment;
- offers some decentralization in social decision-making, but on balance reinforces centralized administration and tends to erode democracy;
- offers potentially to enhance citizen participation in local government, to inform citizens of their rights and duties, and to provide new information-services to citizens, but on balance it reinforces local dominant coalitions, makes local government more expensive to run, makes it less responsive to the general public, and tends to exclude many interests;[20]
- offers potentially more security for data processing and transmission, but on balance threatens privacy in unprecedented ways;
- offers the suggestion of more social equity, but on balance adds to existing social disparities the phenomenon of information inequality.

From these developments stems a new perspective that has recently entered the informatics debate in developed countries: the call for a temporization of informatics applications and even for a 'moratorium' to create the necessary space for the design and realization of policies and institutions through which this technology can be assessed, steered and its negative impact controlled.[21] This makes very questionable a move to propose that developing countries install informatics as rapidly and widely as possible.

Policy questions

– The integration of telecommunication and informatics raises a host of policy questions, its application demands considerable planning and many resources, and necessitates minimally the close coordination between telecommunication and informatics authorities and the users.

Developing countries will have to define precisely which applications of telematics are appropriate, and careful balancing has to be done between limited resources and dubious benefits. These benefits tend to be overestimated due to the hasty equation of advanced data networks with information that is functional to independent economic development. Self-reliance through telematics, however, is not only a matter of the capacity for hardware and/or software production, but even more of the capacity to select and process data into functional information.

Information needs often tend to be defined by technical performance capacity. A crucial question for developing countries is whether they do indeed need the advanced level of information traffic telematics offers.

– The present state of policy formulation and policy implementation in the telematics field leaves a lot to be desired (see Table XIX). Analyzing data from an IBI survey the following picture emerges: developing countries show a tendency to introduce informatics (even with 'imperative' policies) that put stress on the procurement of equipment rather than on the coordination between informatics and telecommunication or computer training. There is little interest to develop national or regional industrial independence, to establish public enterprises or to control foreign enterprises. With the exception of countries in the Asian region there is little interest in public research in the informatics field, as there is generally hardly any interest in joint ventures, control of foreign imports or customs restrictions. Also, there are only in a minority of countries policies regulating transborder data flows or the use of satellites for international communication. The intention to control the negative social impact of informatics is not present in all countries, and legal texts in this context are hardly or not at all in force. Institutional bodies with decision-making power are present in only 22 countries out of the 43 participating in the survey.

Table XIX Informatics Policies in Developing Countries

Region	Africa	Latin America	Asia
Total number of Countries in Survey	18	12	13
Objectives of National Policies			
Procurement of equipment	13	11	13
Informatics-Telecommunication coordination	8	5	10
Computer training in technical and high school	1	7	1
National industrial independence	2	4	5
Regional industrial independence	6	4	6
Establishment public enterprises	2	3	10
Control foreign enterprises	2	0	4
Penalizing foreign enterprises	1	0	2
Public research	6	7	11
Joint ventures	3	4	5
Control of foreign imports	8	3	6
Customs restrictions	5	1	3
Regulation transborder data flow	8	5	7
Control on negative impact	12	6	6
Institutional Arrangements			
Body with decision-making power	8	6	8

Source: Survey on strategy and policies for informatics throughout the world, Intergovernmental Bureau for Informatics, July 1978.

National disintegration

A major problem will be that given the present state of resources, policies and technology, data networks will considerably contribute to national disintegration.

Telematics will primarily promote industrialization in urban areas. Its 'urban bias' will tend to connect such urban-centred industries and thus provide advanced information services to privileged recipients. The telematics market will exclusively benefit the local business class and central administration. The rural and urban low- and middle-income classes will be excluded. This will reproduce the type of information structure the colonial system had imposed. Furthering of national disparities will be the result.

Notes Chapter 7

1 Particularly with reference to microelectronics one finds in the literature an abundant use of such labels as 'the third industrial revolution', 'the new technological revolution', or 'the fundamental transformation of society's structure'. Futurologist Alvin Toffler, in his book *The Third Wave,* New York: Morrow, 1980, claims that the new technologies of our age will bring about social structures radically different from the current ones.

2 Elaborated in C. J. Hamelink, *De Computersamenleving,* Baarn: Anthos, 1980.

3 R. Williams, *Television, Technology and Cultural Form,* London: Fontana, 1974, p 19.

4 J. H. Clippinger, *Who gains by communication development?* Working paper for the Programme on Information Technologies and Public Policy (76–1), Harvard University, January 1976.

5 K. E. Eapen, 'The Cultural Component of SITE', in *The Journal of Communication,* Vol 29 No 4, 1979, p 112.

6 R. E. Jacobson, 'Satellite Business Systems and the Concept of the Dispersed Enterprise: An End to National Sovereignty?', paper for an East-West Communication Institute seminar, Honolulu, 1978, p 30.

7 Commission of the European Communities, *European Society Faced with Challenge of New Information Technologies: A Community Response,* November 26, 1979.

8 R. A. C. Saur, 'Informatics, new technologies and data regulation', paper in *ONLINE, Data Regulation: European and Third World Realities,* Uxbridge, 1978, p 224.

9 H. I. Schiller, *Who Knows: Information in the Age of the Fortune 500,* Norwood: Ablex Publishing, 1981, p 147.

10 Ibidem, p 147.

11 Egypt, for example, intends to expand and improve its telephone network. Contracts have been awarded to Siemens and Thomson-CSF and a European banking consortium provides US\$ 5 billion loan against the security of oil revenues from Sinai and Red Sea exploitations. Ghana, for example, signed in 1981 a US\$ 9.3 million contract with Nippon Electric Company for the Ghanaian part of the Pan African Telecommunications Network.

12 Domestic satellite projects are found in Algeria, Chile, China, Colombia, India, Indonesia, Malaysia, Mauretania, Nigeria, Oman, Peru, the Philippines, Saudi

Arabia, Sudan, Thailand, Uganda, Venezuela and Zaire. Projected regional satellite systems: Arabsat, Andean Satellite System and African Satellite System.

13 For example, for Region 2 (the Americas) allocation of the Ku-Band (11.7–12.26 GHz) which is of particular importance for developing countries (both for broadcast and fixed services) has still to be worked out.

14 In 1981 public data networks are installed i.a. in Chile (by GT&E Telenet) and in Mexico (by GT&E Telenet).

15 L. Pouzin, 'The seven plagues of the 80s', in *Computerworld,* December 8, 1980.

16 S. Nora and A. Minc, *L'informatisation de la société,* Paris: La Documentation Française, 1978, p 72.

17 Average initial costs of a data bank installation are US$ 1 million. Annual expenses average US$ 150,000.

18 Survey on strategy and policies for informatics throughout the world, Intergovernmental Bureau for Informatics, July 1978.

19 Intergovernmental Conference on Strategies and Policies for Informatics, UNESCO-IBI, Torremolinos, August 28–September 6, 1978.

20 See i.a. *Computers and Politics,* Columbia University Press (1982), a study by the Urban Information Systems Research Group, at the University of California Irvine's Public Policy Research Organisation. Data processing applications and their impact on local administration was studied in 42 US cities representative of US local government.

21 H. I. Schiller, o.c., p 149. The issue of a 'moratorium' is discussed in i.a. Australia and the Netherlands.

8 Data Regulation

As can be concluded from the preceding chapters the impact of transnational data flows – although not yet satisfactorily substantiated – raises a number of serious concerns. There is at present an increasing awareness of the need to find adequate responses to these concerns. It seems likely that the search for such responses goes beyond the existing international regulatory framework.

The international community knows a variety of instruments and institutions through which different aspects of information flows are subject to rules of varying specificity, scope and legal strength.

They relate to such areas of international law as freedom of information (human rights), industrial and intellectual property rights, telecommunication law, space law, trade/customs regulations and intergovernmental cooperation.

A number of these regulatory instruments may have implications for transnational data flows and may be stretched to cover certain aspects of electronic data transmissions. They have, however, not been created with this in mind and are not necessarily adequate for all the new and specific concerns involved.[1]

To date, regulatory efforts regarding transnational data flows are couched in the format of national laws, intergovernmental agreements and definitions of future national policies.*

A number of countries have taken steps to formulate and implement laws that have implications for the transmission of digital data across their borders. In almost all cases such laws concentrate solely on person-related data. They have primarily been designed to deal with the concern about the protection of personal data. Their origin stems from the 'informatisation of society': the increasing application of computer technology to data collection, storage and processing. This was seen to possibly lead to such centralized information

* For the present state of data protection legislation, see Table XX.

94

Table XX Status of Data Protection Legislation, January 1982

Country	National	Sub-national	Reports
Australia		L	RP
Austria	L		R
Belgium	(P)		
Canada	L, P	L	R
Denmark	L		R
Finland			RP
France	L		R
Germany	L (P)	L, P	R
Hungary	L		
Iceland	L		
Ireland		RP	
Israel	L		R
Italy			RP
Japan			RP
Luxembourg	L		
Netherlands	(P)		R
New Zealand	L		
Norway	L		R
Portugal	C, P		
Spain	C (P)		R
Sweden	L (P)		R
Switzerland		L	RP
United Kingdom			R
United States	L, P	L	R
Yugoslavia			RP

Code:

L	Law adopted
R	Government report prepared
C	Constitutional Provision
P	Legislation in Parliament
(P)	Draft legislation prepared
RP	Government report in preparation

Source: Transnational Data Report, Vol V No 1, 1982.

control that the privacy of citizens could seriously be endangered. Domestic data protection had to be extended to also cover data exports since national legislation could be evaded by the installation of data processing centres across the border.[2]

West-European countries

The data protection laws that have been adopted during the 1970s in seven West-European countries have several common features.[3]

The most important are:

- they pertain to name-linked data in both public and private computerized files;
- they require licensing or registering of systems for personal data processing;
- they consider all personal data to be sensitive data although special provisions may take care of information for criminal and medical records;
- they establish a national authority as a mechanism for the monitoring and enforcing of the data law;
- they use criminal sanction in case of violation of the law.

An important feature in some laws is the fact that these pertain not only to physical persons, but also to legal persons.[4] The inclusion of legal persons in data protection laws makes it possible to extend restrictions on the transport of data about people, to the exports of data pertaining to legal persons, for example industrial firms or financial institutions.

The notable exception to national regulatory efforts from the perspective of privacy protection is presently Brazil. This country favours the control and restriction of transnational data flows. It opposes the geographical separation between the informational decision-making centre and the data processing location.

It intends to resist manipulation of information by foreign corporations and wants to develop national data banks and other data processing facilities.[5]

The Brazilian regulatory system subjects across-the-border transmission of computer data to national authorization. Such transmission has to comply with the National Policy of Informatics.

Council of Europe and OECD

On the international level attempts have been made to harmonize national legislation into acceptable and coherent international regulation. International agreements that could become common data law for participating parties have been initiated by the Council of Europe and the OECD.[6]

Characteristic of these international agreements is their concentration on flows of personal data. They recognize as a basic principle the free flow of such data across borders but subject them to authorization under certain conditions. Such conditions include national security risks, domestic legislations that bar exports of some categories of sensitive data and transmissions to territories of parties that do not provide protection equivalent to national data legislation.

At present the majority of efforts at data regulation has the format of the definition of national policies. Some 60 countries have adopted forms of national informatics policies. Most of them deal mainly with hardware procurement and priorities for its application. A small number of countries, including Canada, France, Sweden, Algeria, Japan and Brazil have progressed to specifically define transnational data flow policies.

In Canada, for example, the Consultative Committee on the Implications of Telecommunications for Canadian Sovereignty (the so-called 'Clyne' committee) has in its report to the Minister of Communications (end 1979) advised that "The Government should act immediately to regulate transborder data flows so that we do not lose control of information vital to the maintenance of national sovereignty." The report called for data processing related to Canadian business to be executed within Canada, and it proposed an extension of the Bank Act, which already prohibits the exporting of client-linked data for processing and storage abroad in the insurance and loan business.

Surveying the present data regulation scenery, five elements come to the fore:

1 In spite of all present attempts there is no coherent, internationally accepted conceptual framework, and regulation is designed from specific ad-hoc issues. Points of departure for regulatory attempts are such issues as: privacy, national security, national telecommunication policy and national political and economic sovereignty. On the first two issues, there is usually some form of agreement between the parties involved, but the other two yield widely diverging opinions.
2 A survey conducted by *Transnational Data Report* indicates how opinions vary as to regulatory efforts beyond privacy protection. Reacting to the statement that countries should restrict the sending outside their borders of information highly relevant to their economic interests, 39% of the respondents agree, 39% disagree and 21% are undecided.[7]
3 The survey carried out by the Intergovernmental Bureau for Informatics in preparation of the SPIN I Conference (1978) indicated that at the time 35 countries were comtemplating the regulating of transnational data flows. In the absence of a coherent, international, regulatory framework, this is likely

to yield an uncoordinated host of unilateral approaches to transnational data flows.

4 Present regulation tends to cover only part of transnational data transport and processing, and for the totality of data flows there is a regulatory void. Privacy is the focal issue of most present regulation, although transnational data flows also involve volumes of non-person-linked data. At this point, due to lack of empirical data, a clear distribution of personal and non-personal data cannot be given. It is, however, quite possible that in actual fact transnational data flows comprise more person (name)-linked data (e.g. in reservation systems, funds transfers, data base flows and intra-company flows) than one would be inclined to estimate.

5 The adopted regulation for privacy protection may find it difficult to keep pace over the next years with a still further advancing data processing technology. Privacy may confront regulators with totally new dimensions once developments such as electronic funds transfer, electronic mail, the automated office, viewdata and personal computing are in full and wide-scale application.

Issues involved in data regulation

The question as to whether and how transnational data flows should be regulated involves a series of complex issues. Evidently a prime issue is *the protection of privacy*. A clear need has emerged for a legal regime that operates reciprocally among countries or under an international law, and which ensures that person-linked data are handled with respect for the rights of individuals. Such a legal regime would have to compensate the limitations of the national capacity to protect the privacy of national citizens created by transnational data flows. A problem arising here is whether the protection of physical persons should be extended to cover also legal persons. If legal persons are entitled to monitor the data image others hold of them, this could imply access to the files of corporations for competitors, clients and suppliers. The extension could also mean that the range of data for which governmental authorization is needed is extended considerably.

A closely related issue is the application of the principle of *national sovereignty*. This comes up where it is felt that transnational data flows locate crucial social decision-making extraterritorially, erode the possibility to control the conduct of foreign entities on national territory, threaten cultural autonomy, offer inappropriate development models and create dependence on foreign expertise and on political situations in other countries. These can be seen as legitimate political and cultural concerns deserving an adequate legal regime. They can also be seen as issues that relate to national economic concerns to protect domestic industries and to neutralize foreign competition. This brings up the third issue involved in transnational data flow regulation, *domestic economies*. Countries may fear a reduction of employment opportunities because data flows facilitate the transfer of data processing-related jobs. They may also fear that data flows will reduce the utilization of domestic telecommunication facilities because private circuits operating at lower costs will be preferred. They may also desire to protect local data processing facilities against unfair competition caused by disparities in technological development. Against this protection of domestic economies the corporate argument is that government-supported national markets create de facto non-tariff trade barriers and imply unfair trade practices. According to transnational industrialists, the data flow regulation implied in such protection would seriously hamper the operations of large international enterprises (i.e. through time delays in data traffic), would considerably increase their costs (i.e. through restructuring the organisation), and would limit the present flow of goods and services (i.e. through restricting the potential of credit services).

The discussion on the effect of data flow regulation (or deregulation) also has to address the issue of *technological convergence*. With further technological developments all information flows will become digitized. This means that distinctions once based upon distinct technologies will become obsolete. It will be impossible to differentiate between transmissions of news, entertainment or financial data. The question this raises is whether one can regulate transnational data flows without impinging on all the other types of telecommunication traffic.

A last issue deals with the problem of the *implementation of data regulation*. There is the obvious possibility that any regulation that would not be truly international could be evaded through transmitting to and processing in locations – 'data havens' – with considerable leniency towards data protection. More serious seems to be the technical impracticality of control on transnational data flows. Any regulation would have to imply some form of data flow monitoring. The utilization of direct satellite connections, advanced encryption techniques and random routing of fragments of messages will make it practically impossible to control data flows.

Notes Chapter 8

1 "Existing legal regimes do not seem to provide adequate solutions to the specific issues involved. Thus, telecommunication regulation does not deal with the content of messages, neither at the national nor the international level. This branch of communication law can therefore not be used for regulating matters of content which constitute a major aspect of the international rules now being sought, e.g. protection of information on individuals and other sensitive data," argues E. W. Ploman in 'Transborder Data Flows and International Regulation of Information and Communications', a paper for the IBI World Conference on Transborder Data Flow Policies, Rome, June 1980, p 2.

2 Developments in Sweden provide a good illustration. Data regulation was triggered off by concerns about the application of computer technology to data collection, storage and processing. This was seen to possibly lead to such centralized information control that the privacy of citizens could seriously be endangered. To cope with this a Data Act was adopted by the Swedish Parliament in 1973, the first of its kind in the world. Concurrently with the Act a Data Inspection Board was established to control the implementation of the Act. The Data Act protects privacy and gives access to public information. It covers all those personal files operated through automatic data processing and it rules that everyone who wants to create computerized files with data on persons needs a licence. Dealing with the national protection of data quickly turned out to be inadequate. Those who wanted to evade regulation would install their DP centres across the border. Thus, the evasion of national data protection necessitated the restriction of data exports. The Swedish Government made it compulsory to submit all exports of name-linked data to the Data Inspection Board. The principle being that in cases where domestic data protection would be violated data exports had to be restricted.

3 The countries are: Sweden, Federal Republic of Germany, France, Austria, Denmark, Norway and Luxembourg.

4 This is the case in the laws of Austria, Denmark, Norway and Luxembourg.

5 The Brazilian regulatory system became operational in May 1978. The resolution leading to this (by the Coordinating Commission on Data Processing Activities-CAPRE) imposed restrictions on transnational data flows. It established that telematics traffic crossing the national border needs the approval of CAPRE. CAPRE is to guarantee that such traffic does not violate the national information policy. Approval can be given for a maximum of three years. Between May 1979 and early 1980 approval was withheld for the operation of time-sharing services.

6 The major Council of Europe document is the Convention for the Protection of Individuals with regard to Automatic Processing of Personal Data. The Convention was adopted by the Committee of Ministers in Strasbourg, September 1980. The Convention establishes some basic principles for data protection and gives rules to govern transnational data flows.

Article 12 – Transborder flows of personal data and domestic law.
1 The following provisions shall apply to the transfer across national borders, by

whatever medium, of personal data undergoing automatic processing or collected with a view to their being automatically processed.

2 A Party shall not, for the sole purpose of the protection of privacy, prohibit or subject to special authorization transborder flows of personal data going to the territory of another Party.

3 Nevertheless, each Party shall be entitled to derogate from the provisions of paragraph 2:

a) insofar as its legislation includes specific regulations for certain categories of personal data or of automated personal data files, because of the nature of those data or those files, except where the regulations of the other Party provide an equivalent protection;

b) when the transfer is made from its territory to the territory of a non-Contracting State through the intermediary of the territory of another Party, in order to avoid such transfers resulting in circumvention of the legislation of the Party referred to at the beginning of this paragraph.

The OECD Guidelines on Protection of Privacy in Relation to Transborder Flows of Personal Data were adopted by 16 member states in September 1980. The Guidelines give basic principles for personal data protection and for the flow across national borders of such data.

The principle of the free flow of information is crucial. The OECD Council of Ministers has stressed that it is "determined to advance the free flow of information between member countries and to avoid the creation of unjustified obstacles to the development of economic and social relations among member countries." It is recognized, however, that there is a need to reconcile this free-flow principle with the protection of individual privacy. Therefore, there should be space for exceptions on the free-flow principle. The text of the Guidelines reads, "Exceptions to the principles contained in Parts II and III of these Guidelines, including those relating to national sovereignty, national security and public policy ('ordre public'), should be: a) as few as possible; and b) made known to the public." Another restriction is included to help accommodate countries whose domestic legislation bars collection or export of certain types of personal information, except under limited conditions. The wording is as follows: "A member country may also impose restrictions in respect of certain categories of personal data for which its domestic privacy legislation includes specific regulations in view of the nature of those data and for which the other member country provides no equivalent protection."

7 The survey results were reported in *World Survey on Attitudes Regarding Transborder Data Flows,* M. R. Kelly, a paper for the IBI World Conference on Transborder Data Flow Policies, Rome, June 1980.

9 Summary and Considerations for Policy

Summary

In view of the scarcity of presently available empirical research material, it is hardly possible to offer firm conclusions about the political, economic and cultural impact of transnational data flows. Therefore, it seems most appropriate to summarize the main points as they emerge from the preceding discussion particularly on relationships between transnational data flows and their heaviest users, the transnational corporations.

Political, economic and cultural impact can be defined in terms of decisive influence on society's allocation of resources. It has been pointed out that there exists a growing body of documentation that attributes such influence to transnational corporations. In domestic and international economies they are the crucial allocative controllers over volume and direction of important resources. Their processing capacity influences the allocation of natural resources. Their productive capacity influences the allocation of human resources. Their financial capacity influences the allocation of financial resources. Their R&D capacity influences the allocation of scientific/technical resources.

All these dimensions of corporate organisation and operation relate to the resource 'data'. Corporate processing capacity is linked with the collecting of data. Financial and productive capacity are linked with the transporting of data. R&D capacity is linked with processing and storing of data. Transnational corporations can thus be described as 'data-centred'. Their allocative control is closely related to their capacity to access data, to transform data into information/knowledge and to apply data and information/knowledge.

Transnational data flows are an advanced form of data transport and data processing, and at present it seems safe to assume that transnational corporations are their largest users. They can mobilize the financial resources for the hardware, software and transmission costs involved in the use of data flows. They can also mobilize the analytical skill and the networks through which data can be most effectively used.

Transnational data flows will therefore most likely find their strongest impact through their use by transnational corporations, particularly in the following fields:

- increase in operational efficiency and effectiveness of transnational corporations leading to their greater capacity to influence allocation of resources;
- increase in competitive advantage for the largest users leading to their increasing market control;
- contribution to the informatisation of societies;
- increase of informational disparities, nationally and internationally;
- increase of allocative control of transnational corporations vis-à-vis national governments;
- erosion of political and economic sovereignty of national governments, in particular of developing countries;
- furthering of global cultural synchronization;
- hampering of self-reliant development of developing countries.

From the current pattern of international economic and technological disparities follows a differential access to the collecting and analyzing of data and to the mobilization of resources for the utilization of data and information that puts certain actors (such as developing countries) at a disadvantage on world markets.

The differential access to the process of information management causes a sharp disparity between information-dependent and information-independent actors. Information dependence is the situation in which most developing countries find themselves. They are without the national capabilities to meet their data collecting, processing and application requirements. This is felt to compromise their national sovereignty. It locates the capacity to decisively influence the deployment of their resources extraterritorially with information-independent actors. The latter actors have more access to the essential elements of information management and by consequence more impact on political and economic decision-making.

Vis-à-vis resource allocative decisions that affect their economies, the majority of developing countries has very limited capacity to exert influence. Present information discrepancies are likely to primarily benefit the transnational corporations. In bargaining with them much will depend, for developing countries, on their access to information. In negotiating situations the extent of access to and input of information is an important factor of power.

Transnational corporations have a degree of analytical skill, interpretative expertise and access to networks for the processing of data into information and its application in resource management that far outweighs the informational capacity of most developing countries.

If the impact of transnational data flows can indeed be described in such terms as the above, then present data regulation would seem rather insufficient. The following could be indicated as its main deficiencies:

- it is mainly national and unilateral;
- it lacks a comprehensive, coherent conceptual framework;
- it is strongly privacy-oriented;
- it does not take into account future technological advancements.

It is most likely that developing countries will on the one hand want to speed up the introduction of data-flow-related technology in order to reap its potential benefits, and on the other hand will want to avoid its potential deleterious effects on their autonomy. In the weighing of costs against benefits, data regulation in some form is likely to be demanded by developing countries. If, as seems quite logical – due to technological convergences – data flows are viewed as a component of international communication structures, regulation will be directed towards a greater and more autonomous capacity for developing countries for participation in these structures.

Policy

There is an increasing awareness that on national, regional and international levels policies have to be formulated, implemented and evaluated with regard to transnational data flows. The problem with this is that sufficient empirical evidence for an analysis of costs versus benefits is missing, so making clear guidelines for data policies possible. Satisfactory policy-making would have to be based upon research that still has to be done.

Presently one could, however, suggest looking at data flows as an additional component of international communication structures, and deal with them in the context of the emerging national communication/information policies. Throughout the 1970s international and regional conferences have stressed the need for national communication/information policies. The decade ahead will have to see their formulation, implementation and evaluation. Such policies will have to be integrated, i.e. encompass both the more established type of media (such as press and broadcasting) and the more advanced media (such as computer networks). The essential criterion for national communication/information policy-making will have to be the objective of self-reliant development. This means that policy-making will start with defining the function of communication/information systems in the light of overall developmental objectives. The second step will be the critical inventory of indigenous resources that can be exploited or foreign resources that can be imported without undue dependence. Objectives and resources have to be translated into national production and distribution structures. A control mechanism has to be designed for the monitoring of system performance.

Although no complete blueprint could be provided giving all the implications for transborder data flows, the leading questions for policy-making are:

- how does telematics contribute to society's functions? (Will it further national disintegration? Will it introduce inadequate techniques, symbols and social structures?);
- how will telematics relate to resources? (Are it imported? Will this jeopardise national self-reliance?);
- how will telematics be structured? (Can a national production structure be organised?);
- how will telematics be controlled? (Can the import and export of computer data be regulated? Can taxes be imposed on data flows?)

International policy

International policy-making in the field of transnational data flows could direct itself to the role of transnational corporations by adopting a paragraph on data flows in the projected United Nations Code of Conduct for Transnational Corporations. This paragraph would link the data issue with such crucial concerns as the disclosure of information, employment problems, financial transactions, and the transfer of technology.

This would be quite logical since these topics can be seen as indeed 'data-centred'.

- *disclosure of information:* demanding the identification and assessment of volume and direction of corporate participation in host economies, implies access to data flows;
- *employment and labour:* this section would take into account the effects of data flow use on employment opportunities;
- *financing:* control over corporate financial transactions is in fact control over data-flows;
- *transfer of technology:* this can in fact be dealt with as transfer of data, transformed into information/knowledge.

Alongside international policy measures, developing countries in particular could attempt to define regional arrangements.

Regional policy

In response to the fact that hardly any progress has been achieved in spite of years of global negotiations on international economic disparities, strategies of regionalism have been proposed as a means to establish a new international economic order. Despite its rather unsuccessful history, regionalism could indeed be attempted anew as an instrument for more self-reliance and autonomy.

Regional data-flow policy would have to concentrate on the establishment of horizontal networks for the transfer and sharing of resources, the exchange of experiences and the development of joint ventures. The movement towards greater technical cooperation (TCDC) needs to pay special attention to data-processing-related technology and needs to be supported by an efficient and effective infrastructure for the exchange of information on a South-to-South basis.

Fundamental to achieving meaningful measures on the international and regional policy will be the development of the national capacity for comprehensive technology assessment.

Technology assessment and national policy

Technology assessment should comprise the total process of evaluation, distribution, application and production of technical information/knowledge. Technology assessment is the processing of 'technology about technology'.

The development of technology assessment capacity needs the sharing (among developing countries) of knowledge. Not only of technical knowledge, but of an holistic package encompassing know-how of traditional techniques, anthropological, economic, and juridical insights, methodologies of policy analysis, and epistemological tools.

Vis-à-vis this transfer of knowledge, the concept of 'appropriate' – often used in technology debates – is definitely 'inappropriate', since it presents an undue restriction. In constructing the capacity for selection, access to the widest possible body of knowledge is an absolute prerequisite. How appropriate certain technical information and its application are, can only be assessed after ample consultation of the largest variety of sources possible. Once the technology assessment capacity has been secured, 'appropriate technology' becomes a tautology.

The development of comprehensive technology assessment capacity demands national and regional training programmes, the sharing of training resources and experiences among developing countries, and adequate international support in material and intellectual resources.

In order for technology assessment to become operational and functional it needs structural support through national policies and their implementation and monitoring by adequate institutional bodies.

Policies should integrate formerly distinct fields such as planning for general technology, informatics, telecommunication, mass media and patent law.

Policies should define information needs and priorities and balance telematics applications with available resources. Policies should make projections regarding secondary impacts of advanced information technology.

Policies should incorporate the transfer of technical information between countries with comparable levels of technological development.

Policies should adjust existing patent law to become an adequate instrument of national policy.

The institutional arrangements for implementation and evaluation of policies should be public institutions which have technology assessment capacity, which can monitor technological applications, and initiate and control innovations.

They should have decision-making power. They should guard the democratic quality of the technology assessment procedure.

Epilogue

This book has described a salient feature of the imminent information age: the transnational flow of digital data.

This data flow has become possible through the application of important innovations in computer and telecommunication technology.

Particularly, the dazzling speed of the development of these innovations has promoted the belief in the 'technological fix': the conviction that there are technical solutions for all social problems.

The 'fix' is however 'fiction', since technical solutions and social problems are by no means inseparable twins, certainly not when technological developments are steered by narrowly defined private interests. Technological development is not an autonomous process that shapes the politico-economic order of the society in which its results are applied. Technological development responds to the hierarchy of social needs as they are defined by the existing politico-economic order. In preparing for the information age it must be realized that technology in itself is not the crucial problem; rather it is the quality of the definition of social needs.

Given the rapidity of developments and the immense interests at stake, the information age will urgently need to establish the primacy of public policy over private technology. A 'laissez faire, laissez aller' approach towards telematics technology leaves the critical decisions for the information age to private interests and is likely to further aggravate the world's most pressing problem: the unequal distribution of its vital resources.

Planning for the information age does recognize the fact that technology should be steered by public interests and respond to democratically defined social needs.

List of Tables

Bibliography

R. Alloway, *Decision Support Systems and Information Flow in the 80s,* in E. J. Boutmy and A. Danthine (eds.), *Teleinformatics '79,* Amsterdam: North Holland, 1979, pp 3–8.

G. Anderla, *Information in 1985,* Paris, OECD, 1973.

J. Becker, *Euro-American Conflicts in the Sphere of Transborder Data Flow,* paper prepared for the conference on 'Culture and Communication', Temple University, Philadelphia, April 9–11, 1981.

D. Bell, *The Coming of Post-Industrial Society,* New York: Basic Books, 1976.

M. Benedetti, *Eurodata '79: the growth of data communications in West Europe,* paper for the IBI World Conference on Transborder Data Flow Policies, Rome, June 1980.

A. R. Berkeley, *Millionaire Machine?,* in *Datamation,* August 25, 1981, pp 20–36.

P. A. Blesch, *Developing Countries' Exports of Electronics and Electrical Engineering Products,* Washington: World Bank, 1978.

J. P. Chamoux, *L'information sans frontière,* Paris: La Documentation Française, 1980.

J. H. Clippinger, *Who gains by communication development?* Working paper for the Programme on Information Technologies and Public Policy (76–1), Harvard University, January 1976.

Commission of the European Communities, *European Society Faced with Challegne of New Information Technologies: A Community Response,* November 26, 1979.

X. Dalloz and P. Grandperret, *Les chiffres-clés de l'Informatisation,* Paris: La Documentation Française, 1980.

M. Disman, *Software Trends in Europe,* in *Datamation,* August 25, 1981, pp 41–48.

H. S. Dordick, H. G. Bradley and B. Nanus, *The Emerging Network Marketplace,* Norwood: Ablex Publishing, 1981.

K. E. Eapen, *The Cultural Compnent of SITE,* in *The Journal of Communication,* Vol 29 No 4, 1979.

A. S. Edelstein, J. E. Bowes, S. M. Harsel (eds), *Information Societies: Comparing the Japanese and American Experiences,* Seattle, International Communication Centre, School of Communications, University of Washington, 1978.

H. L. Freeman and J. E. Spiro, *Services are the Major Issue of the 1980s,* in *Transnational Data Report,* Vol IV No 7, 1981.

J. Freese, *International Data Flow,* Lund: Studentlitteratur, 1979.

A. Gotlieb, Ch. Dalfen, and K. Katz, *The Transborder Transfer of Information by Communications and Computer Systems,* in *The American Journal of International Law,* Vol 68 No 2, April 1974, pp 227–257.

C. J. Hamelink, *The Corporate Village,* Rome: IDOC, 1977.

C. J. Hamelink, *Cultural Autonomy in Global Communications,* New York: Longman, 1983.

C. J. Hamelink, *Finance and Information,* Norwood: Ablex Publishing, 1983.

D. Hebditch, *Will data flow be stemmed?,* in *Telecommunications,* May 1979.

E. F. M. Hogrebe, *Digital Technology: The Potential for Alternative Communication,* in *Journal of Communication,* Vol 31 No 1, 1981, pp 170–176.

F. W. Hondius, *Emerging data protection in Europe,* Amsterdam: North Holland, 1975.

S. Horwitz, *On the Road to Wired City,* in *Harvard Magazine,* September/October 1979, pp 18–19.

Ph. Hughes and R. Sasson, *Development of Data Networks in Europe,* paper in *ONLINE, Data Regulation: European and Third-World Realities,* Uxbridge, 1978.

Intergovernmental Bureau for Informatics, *World Conference on Transborder Data Flow Policies,* final proceedings, Rome, October 1980.

International Commission for the Study of Communication Problems, *Many Voices, One World,* Paris: UNESCO, 1980.

R. E. Jacobson, *Satellite Business Systems and the Concept of the Dispersed Enterprise: An End to National Sovereignty?,* paper for an East-West Communication Institute seminar, Honolulu, 1978.

H. Katzan, *Multinational Computer Systems,* New York: Van Nostrand Reinhold Company, 1980.

M. R. Kelly, *World Survey on Attitudes regarding Transborder Data Flows,* Paper for the IBI World Conference on Transborder Data Flow Policies, Rome, June 1980.

A. D. Little, *The Netherlands in the Information Age,* The Hague: Centrum voor Informatiebeleid, 1981.

Logica Ltd., *The Usage of International Data Networks in Europe,* Paris: OECD, 1979.

A. J. Madec, *Economic and Legal Aspects of Transborder Data Flow,* paper for the High Level Conference on Information, Computer and Communication Policies in the 1980s, Paris: OECD, October 1980.

S. Nora and A. Minc, *L'informatisation de la société,* Paris: La Documentation Française, 1978.

OECD, *The role of information goods and services in international trade,* paper prepared for the OECD working party on Information, Computer and Communications Policy, Paris, May 1979.

A. G. Oettinger, (and others), *Foreign Policy Choices for the 1970s and 1980s,* Cambridge (MA): Harvard University Programme on Information Technologies and Public Policy, 1976.

E. W. Ploman, *Transborder Data Flows and International Regulation of Information and Communications,* paper for IBI World Conference on Transborder Data Flow Policies, Rome, June 1980.

M. U. Porat, *The Information Economy: Definition and Measurement,* Washington (DC): US Department of Commerce/Office of Telecommunications, 1977.

J. F. Rada, *Some Issues and Possibilities posed by the Unfolding Information Revolution,* document DEC/D/75/i, Mexico: ILET, 1980.

M. D. Ripper and J. L. C. Wanderley, *The Brazilian Computer and Communications Regulatory Environment and Transborder Data Flow Policy,* paper for the IBI World Conference on Transborder Data Flow Policies, June 1980.

P. Robinson, *The Economic Impact of TDF,* paper for the IBI World Conference on Transborder Data Flow Policies, Rome, June 1980.

S. Rose, *The unexpected fallout from electronic banking,* in *Fortune,* April 24, 1978.

R. A. C. Saur, *Informatics, new technologies and data regulation,* paper in *ONLINE, Data Regulation: European and Third-World Realities,* Uxbridge, 1978, pp 223–233.

L. Siegel, *Microelectronics does little for the Third World,* in *The Microelectronic Wave,* IDOC Bulletin No 1–2, Rome: IDOC, 1981.

B. Silverman, *International Telecommunications as a Tool for Technology Transfer,* paper for Technology I. Exchange '78, Atlanta, February 9, 1978.

I. de Sola Pool and J. Solomon, *Intellectual property and transborder data flows,* in *Stanford Journal of International Law,* Summer 1980, pp 113–139.

A. Tenkoff, *Transborder Data Flow – what are the issues?* Paper for the International Conference on Transnational Data Flows, Washington, December 1979.

J. M. Treille, *New Strategies for Business Information,* Paris: OECD, document DSTI/ICCP/79, March 1979.

R. Turn, (ed.), *Transborder Data Flows,* Arlington (VA): American Federation of Information Processing Societies, 1979.

United Nations Centre on Transnational Corporations, *Transnational Corporations and Transborder Data Flows,* document ST/CTC/23, New York, 1981.

R. H. Veith, *Multinational Computer Nets,* Lexington (MA): D. C. Heath, 1982.

P.I. van Velse, *Aspects of a European Information Industry,* paper for the Commission of the European Communities, Luxembourg, September 5, 1979.

J. A. Viera-Gallo, *Documentation for Change,* report for the meeting of documentation centres on Third-World issues, Lisbon, January, 1982.

Subject Index

INFORMATION AND SOCIETY SERIES

The impact of computer technology on society is growing rapidly. The need for understanding and debate is enormous. This new series, coordinated by Transnational Data Reporting Service, Inc (TDRS), is one essential step. The series is edited by Jan Freese, chairman of the Swedish Data Inspection Board and an internationally well-known expert on the question of computers and society, and G. Russell Pipe, editorial director, TDRS.

Becker, Jörg, editor
Information Technology and a New International Order

Information technology, which has resulted in Telematics and Transborder Data Flows is quickly becoming part of the North-South dialogue – or conflict. Many of the political, social-cultural and economic aspects of this issue are presented in the book.

Hamelink, Cees J
Transnational Data Flows in the Information Age

This study is about the most potent form of telecommunication: transnational data flows. It sets out to describe the main actors and their impact on society. The context of the analysis is the information age: the recognition that information is becoming the most operative factor of society.

Freese, Jan
Vulnerability or Robustness in the Computerized Society

Modern technological, import and export depending society was already before computerisation very vulnerable. The new technology has made the margins still more narrow. The book presents how to make society robust again.

Freese, Jan – Pipe, Russel
Privacy Laws and Computerized Information

More and more countries legislate in the field of privacy and computers. The book presents the different privacy laws as well as the result of national cooperation in OECD and the Council of Europe.